HISTORIC CHRONICLES
of GENESEE COUNTY

HISTORIC CHRONICLES
of GENESEE COUNTY

MICHAEL J. EULA

THE
History
PRESS

Published by The History Press
Charleston, SC
www.historypress.com

All images courtesy of the Genesee County History Department Archives.

First published 2024

Manufactured in the United States

ISBN 9781467156738

Library of Congress Control Number: 2023950896

Notice: The information in this book is true and complete to the best of our knowledge. It is offered without guarantee on the part of the author or The History Press. The author and The History Press disclaim all liability in connection with the use of this book.

For my wife, Allie, without whom I could not have written this book.

CONTENTS

PREFACE

Was it not in the close mesh of local experience that great national events themselves acquired a felt reality…
—John Higham, History: Professional Scholarship in America

In this quote, Professor Higham is referring to the classic work of Robert A. Gross, *The Minutemen and Their World.*[1] Gross examined the Revolutionary War through the eyes of people in Concord, Massachusetts. The Revolution, a national event, played out locally in a multitude of ways. The people of Concord lived in a local universe shaped by national developments. They did not live in a world disconnected from issues arising elsewhere.

The work of Gross reminds us that the history of the United States did not take place solely on the national level. I have long thought that this is true outside the Concord Gross wrote about. My work in Genesee County, New York, intensified that feeling. From the formation of the county in 1802 on, Genesee County's culture remained inextricably bound to national events. In turn, that local culture shaped the perception of national developments. I contend that the culture of Genesee County, a rural area in western New York, has been one consistently linked with national life. To understand more fully the national development of the United States, one must spend time with a specific local area. Hence this book.

Genesee County's story began with its formation from Ontario County on March 30, 1802. "Genesee" was a reference to a Seneca Native American word, *gen-nis-ye-ho,* meaning "beautiful valley." As the county's population

A 1901 postcard showing the Holland Land Office in Batavia.

grew, eight counties nearby were formed in the years between 1806 and 1841. These included Allegany, Cattaraugus, Chautauqua, Erie (from Niagara), Orleans, Wyoming, and the western sections of Monroe and Livingston. Today, the county contains thirteen towns, six villages, and a city. The city, Batavia, serves as the county seat in a county with a total population of 58,288, as of the 2020 U.S. Census.

This largely rural county was the result of the work of Dutch bankers from the Holland Land Company who, in 1792, oversaw the work of its land agent, Joseph Ellicott, who subdivided the land through land sales commencing in November 1800. Batavia was selected as the county seat because of its location on the Buffalo Road, while its name was selected to pay tribute to the short-lived Dutch Republic.[2]

Over time, the county's population grew along with its economy—an economy that remained primarily agricultural. The second half of the twentieth century exhibited the greatest spurt of growth in the history of the county, as industries such as O-At-Ka Milk Products and Sylvania Electric commenced operations. Between 1940 and 1970, the 31 percent increase in county population reflected the growing demand for labor, both agricultural and industrial. Nevertheless, agriculture remained the county's economic foundation, with more than half of the county's acreage devoted to farming.[3] However, despite these changes, a central theme in the county's history remained.

Accordingly, national developments manifested themselves locally. Conversely, local developments indicated the direction of national trends. Patterns on one level did not exclude patterns on the other. These patterns are discernible in such areas of county life as newspapers and social movements. An event such as the New Deal in Genesee County only emerged because of the New Deal taking place nationally. Newspapers reporting on such developments as New Deal programs filtered these national stories through a local lens. The interplay of developments on two levels is one consistently emphasized throughout this short book. Readers looking for a chronology of county events devoid of this complex interaction will be disappointed, for this is not a simple chronological narrative.

Therefore, I selected topics revealing the relationship between local and national developments—what I call "Chronicles"—and how this interplay affected county life. I also selected topics that have been overlooked in the local literature, such as the Cold War, assassinations, and the New Deal. As a result, this book contains six chapters representing the main currents of the county's historical stream, currents not taken up in some of the other local literature.[4] Our journey takes us from national leaders stretching back to President John F. Kennedy, into the construction of ethnicity and then the New Deal and on into realities faced by women in Genesee County. By no means do the six chapters I have included exhaust all of the vastness of the county's past. Nonetheless, they do help us see the major themes of county, and national, history between 1802 and our own day. However, much more work is needed.

What I have done represents an effort to illustrate how some of those national and local patterns merged. I selected topics based on the availability of sources and the interests of people with whom I have spoken with during my nine years as Genesee County Historian. County archives and the interests of the public in Genesee County, evident in dozens of public talks and among visitors working in the county archives, allow me to conclude that there are five themes in the county's history that dominate historical thinking locally. These include an interest in public figures, particularly those who suffered early deaths. Secondly, war dominates local thinking about the importance of the past. Thirdly, what I think of as identities compels reflection about what it means to live in Genesee County as an immigrant and then as a descendant of immigrants. Fourthly, social movements, such as the New Deal, produced much discussion about the role of government in county life. National developments sometimes produced sinister reactions, as we shall see in the discussion of the growth of the Ku Klux Klan. Finally, archival sources and public interest prompted my discussion of how women in the county helped shape the culture and institutions of county life from the nineteenth century on.

These themes capture the interaction of national and local developments. In chapter 1, the national event of assassinations resonated locally, as we shall see. The complex interplay between the county and the nation at large during the Cold War is illustrated by the preparedness drill of 1956, discussed in Chapter 2. In Chapter 3, we see how identity as a county resident was refashioned by immigration in the nineteenth and early twentieth centuries. In Chapter 4, I examine the national policies created by the Great Depression and the New Deal, how these policies were received locally, and how those local sentiments modified the perception of those programs. National policies regarding such issues as immigration and Prohibition induced local reactions, as was evident in the rise of the Ku Klux Klan in the early 1920s, a topic presented in chapter 5. Readers will also discover realities faced by women in the county's history as well as how national developments played a part in the history of women in the county. Those issues arising in women's history in the county form the basis of Chapter 6.

It is hoped that readers with an interest in local history, Genesee County, or otherwise, will find this to be a stimulating and informative book.[5] Those with an interest in the history of the United States can see how one area of the country fits into the wider national picture. Genesee County's past, like those of other locales, constitutes one of many watersheds in what is ultimately a national story with many local variations.

This book owes much to others. Professor Elliot Rosen at Rutgers initially sparked an interest in history that never waned. My graduate professors, especially Professor David J. Pivar, nurtured that spark in the years I studied at California State University–Fullerton and the University of California–Irvine. The historical societies of Genesee County encouraged me to see the importance of local history through the example of their work. My colleagues at the Genesee County History Department, Judy Stiles and Ruth Koch, provided continuous and necessary staff support. Adam Doktor of the Genesee County IT Department provided needed technical support. J. Banks Smither of The History Press provided much editorial support. His patience and comments facilitated the completion of this project. Finally and most importantly, my wife, Allison, sustained me with love, devotion, and endless patience, especially during a protracted illness. I could not have written this book without Allie.

CHAPTER 1

IN ONLY SIX YEARS

GENESEE COUNTY REACTS TO THE ASSASSINATIONS OF THE KENNEDYS AND MARTIN LUTHER KING JR.

It seemed that only death awaited young men of vision and energy.
—David W. Noble et al., Twentieth Century Limited

The 1960s were a tumultuous time in the United States. A number of forces converged to produce visible cracks in what appeared to be, at first glance, a post–World War II society of shared values. Despite the expanding prosperity of the period, there was, simultaneously, a growing unease concerning income inequality and poverty—both urban and rural. However, for those who remembered the Great Depression and World War II, it was all too easy to reject the need for reform and experimentation in lieu of an enjoyment of affluence (at least for some) and security. Nonetheless, many of the baby boom generation, not remembering the Great Depression and World War II, were quick to remind America of the gap between the perception of affluence and the reality of poverty. In addition, other developments compelled many to acknowledge that life is not always reducible to security, predictability, and a joy rooted in abundance. These developments took place in a six-year period between 1963 and 1968. As one article in the *Daily News* put it in the wake of the assassination of President John F. Kennedy in November 1963, "Even for a generation that had known such events as Pearl Harbor, the death of Franklin D. Roosevelt, D-Day, victory days of World War II, and Korea, this [President Kennedy's assassination] was a new and frightening experience." This same article, headlined "Normalcy Returning to Area after President's Funeral, Many Attend Rites in City," included the following: "Something akin to normalcy returned to the Batavia area today as residents began to emerge from the cloud of unreality of a tragic weekend....That the shock of the events since Friday had not worn off was evident as residents went through the mechanics of their daily jobs, but with less enthusiasm than usual."[6]

This and other *Daily News* articles demonstrated the shock that the Kennedy assassination caused in the local community. Quite unexpectedly—and especially for those enjoying greater affluence and security—the death of President Kennedy was a reminder that America's good life could very quickly change into something featuring unpredictability and senselessness. Material abundance could not erase the deeper anxieties of modern America. The subsequent assassinations of Senator Robert F. Kennedy in June 1968 and Dr. Martin Luther King Jr. the previous April also underlined the suddenness with which change could occur—a shift not always amounting to a better future.

In this chapter, we explore the impact and underlying meaning of the assassinations of three of the period's pivotal American leaders in Genesee County. As conveyed in innumerable county media accounts, these killings undermined assumptions about life in America and weakened optimism and hope. For example, a June 8, 1968, editorial in the *Daily News* commented on Senator Robert Kennedy's assassination, "Is America 'sick?' That is a phrase that is being bandied about with some abandon in recent years in the wake of violence, assassinations and other demonstrations that actually are not of the American tradition. To be sure, America is not perfect. But it is sincerely striving to improve—a factor that undoubtedly generates some of the heat that becomes abrasive and disturbing to some and kindles explosions." The writer continued, "It is better that there is this effort and attitude rather than complacency and acceptance of [the] status quo which, in the long run, would be far more devastating."[7]

As this editorial reminds us, it was increasingly difficult to ignore the fractures evident in American society. The suddenness of all three assassinations made the routine of daily life seem more precarious than ever. In all three cases, both nationally and in Genesee County, other consequences appeared. The capacity of the modern media was evident and commented on repeatedly. Modern media quickly broadcast the news, making these assassinations national and international events almost instantaneously, bringing normal daily life to a virtual standstill—and, in the case of King, prompting even violent reactions.

The youthful energy of both of the Kennedys and of King remained inseparable from the sudden appearance of death. Their deaths at relatively young ages, combined with the energy displayed in their public images, reminded many of their own mortality, which no amount of success and material affluence could overcome. As the *Daily News* reminded its readers following King's death, his vitality translated into his being "a man of courage and depth who stood for what he believed [in] at the risk of personal humiliation and worse."[8]

The deaths of these national figures also brought into focus another aspect of Cold War life: the pervasive and yet unspoken fear of nuclear war. The sudden deaths of these leaders condensed the possibility of mass death to more comprehensible human proportions. The Kennedys and King embodied the sudden death that could come for anyone. Each American, like these three, was vulnerable. This perspective put much of American life into a new light—a theme apparent in the county's reaction to these assassinations.

Four themes, then, are discernible in Genesee County's reaction to these assassinations. These include the crucial role played by modern communications. This led to the forging of a common experience that united people and brought their lives to a momentary halt. The images accentuated the stark contrast between the youthful energy of all three murdered leaders and their sudden and violent deaths. Discernible as well was the palpable fear of mass death in a nuclear age that that was prompted by the three killings. These killings reduced mass, anonymous death to something more personable, something more comprehensible. During this period, media became so pervasive that it not only recorded pivotal events such as these three assassinations, it also functioned to facilitate historical change. The 1960s ushered in electronic changes that had started in earlier years but that now accelerated because of the technology available. Watching these events and their aftermath on television created not just observers—it created participants. To view the assassination of President Kennedy's alleged assassin, Lee Harvey Oswald, was to *participate* in the creation of a decisive historical moment, an experience not possible for millions of people before the advent of live television broadcasts.

Also evident—although this aspect of the public's reaction is not explored in this chapter—is a skepticism that the lives of such leaders could not have been so abruptly ended by lone gunmen, be it Lee Harvey Oswald, Sirhan Sirhan or James Earl Ray. A group with something to gain from these deaths must have planned and coordinated each killing. The important point here is the role of perception rather than factual accuracy. The view that slowly but surely took hold in Genesee County—as it did throughout the United States—was that these crimes were so far-reaching in their consequences that they could not have resulted from the actions of lone gunmen. Embedded in American culture—for reasons that take us beyond the scope of this chapter—is the idea that sinister developments in highly dramatic moments such as these suggest coordination from lofty levels of power.

It is simply not satisfying for many to embrace the idea that a lone gunman acted out of mental illness or even ideological fervor. Instead, it is more comforting to conclude that an intricate web of murderers was trying to stop the plans of a great leader. We want to believe that a leader died as the victim of opposition to a cause rather than at the hands of an unbalanced assassin. As the following excerpt from the *Daily News* reminds us, the Warren Commission's efforts were, for many, unconvincing. Keep in mind that this assessment of the assassination of President Kennedy, released to the public on September 27, 1964, totaled twenty-six volumes. It included hundreds of thousands of pages of documents and investigative reports and 8,082 pages of testimony. Commission members took affidavits, testimonies or statements from 552 witnesses—more than ten times the number of witnesses who appeared before the joint Congressional committee that investigated the attack on Pearl Harbor. The Federal Bureau of Investigation conducted twenty-five thousand interviews as the investigatory arm of the Warren Commission, while 3,154 pieces of evidence were introduced before this commission.[9] Nonetheless, the *Daily News* expressed the doubts of many Americans about the Warren Commission's report in a September 30, 1964 editorial: "The great unanswered question in the report of the Warren Commission—which has just concluded that Lee Harvey Oswald killed President John F. Kennedy—is why he did it. The seven-man commission, headed by Chief Justice Earl Warren, after almost 10 months of investigation and with the help of all the resources of government, admits it couldn't learn Oswald's reason for the assassination."[10] The inability to identify motive, this editorial argued, meant that many other questions also remained unanswered. One of these questions was whether Oswald acted alone.

With all of this in mind, then, we turn first to the murder of President Kennedy and the reaction it produced in Genesee County.

THE ASSASSINATION OF PRESIDENT KENNEDY

As is well known, President Kennedy was shot and killed in Dallas on November 22, 1963. Ironically, the same media that had played a major role in his rise to the White House now captured—and rapidly spread—news of his death. A few days later, it also conveyed the images of his funeral and—to add to the shock of his sudden death on that Friday in November—the shooting, broadcast live, of his alleged assassin, Lee Harvey Oswald, in the basement of the Dallas Police Department by Jack Ruby.

There is little doubt that television coverage deepened the impact of the assassination on the public. To sit before the television screen for several days in a row was to absorb gripping images. The horrors of the events contrasted with the vibrant images of a young president and his even younger wife—and their small children—with which Americans had become familiar. For instance, shots of Mrs. Kennedy at public events in happier times combined with the image of her in bloodstained clothes.

Such horrific depictions, contrasted with those of normal days, produced a common experience that translated into a virtual halt of everyday life in the days following November 22. This was as true in Genesee County as it was throughout the rest of the nation. Only one day after the assassination, the front page of the *Daily News* featured the headline "Shock and Disbelief Mark News of the Assassination as Batavians Learn of Death."[11] Several pages into that same issue, indicating just how fast the news spread, we see an article titled "Shock Wave of President Kennedy's Death Engulfs High and Low throughout World." Readers were informed that the "tragic flash from Dallas reverberated around the world like a clap of thunder: the young vigorous President of the United States was dead…and everywhere the great and the lowly mourned John F. Kennedy's passing."[12]

Not surprisingly, the grief felt around the world was, the paper reported, "clearly evident in Genesee County as well." The news spread swiftly through Batavia. Within the hour, "everyone on Main St. knew what had happened." The same November 23 article quoted numerous people articulating similar feelings of shock—a shared experience both within and beyond Genesee County, intensified by the role played by a media capable of disseminating news very quickly. One woman, identified only as "Mrs. Kelso," was "in the C.L. Carr Store when she heard the news." She said, "It was a terrible shock. I had just read about the President and his son in *Look* magazine. He called his son, John, John. This doesn't seem possible." Harold A. Craig, the mayor of Alexander, "found it difficult to control his emotions." He told the *Daily*

News reporter, "I am terribly shocked." A police officer who walked a beat on Batavia's Main Street, Lawrence Falkowski, commented that the news was "hard to believe." The *Daily News* concluded, "This was the reaction on Main St. Within the hour of the news of the assassination of the President people found it difficult to believe such a thing could happen in America."[13]

But it had happened, and it produced a virtual standstill in ordinary life. Readers learned that on the day of the president's funeral, Monday, November 25, the New York Stock Exchange would remain closed, while locally schools were closed, the Batavia High School senior play was rescheduled "for a later date"[14] and stores closed until 2:00 p.m.[15] Normal television programming was suspended until Tuesday, November 26, while networks focused exclusively on the assassination, funeral, and related events.[16] It was not until that Tuesday, November 26, that the *Daily News* could feature a front-page article capturing this shift: "Normalcy Returning to Area after President's Funeral, Many Attend Rites in City Tragic Weekend Comes to Close, Business Resumes."[17]

Yet despite the depiction of relative normalcy, the stark contrast between a youthful President Kennedy and the suddenness of his death abounded. For instance, on the very last page of the *Daily News* only a day before, the Ryan-DeWitt Corporation sponsored a full-page statement. Half of this page showed a photograph of a young and purposeful President Kennedy followed by the caption: "In Memory of Our Beloved President John Fitzgerald Kennedy 'A Profile in Courage'" (a reference to the book published only a few years earlier by then Senator Kennedy).[18]

Over the next several days, the images of youthful energy stood in stark contrast to the president's funeral. This contrast extended to his widow. On November 26, the *Daily News* featured a front-page article headlined "At Midnight, Mrs. Kennedy Goes to Husband's Grave with a Sprig of Flowers." Reminding readers that Jacqueline Kennedy was "a widow at 34," the article reported that even someone as prominent as the president's widow could have the security of her position suddenly, and senselessly, swept away: "Among the foremost questions are how long will she remain at the White House, where will she make her new home and what will become of the White House school she set up for daughter Caroline and some 20 other children."[19]

Why was this contrast between youthful life and death particularly poignant in 1963, reaching a frenzied level with the Kennedy assassination? The short answer is the presence of a death anxiety in American life. A widely read book titled *The American Way of Death* became a bestseller in that same year.[20] Jessica Mitford's work stressed that Americans employed a variety of tactics to avoid the reality that life is finite. She asserted that funeral directors designed methods that facilitated covering up bodily disintegration and gruesome wounds. However, President Kennedy's wounds were too extensive to be covered. He was simply, and irrevocably, dead, and his casket remained closed.

His literal annihilation went straight to the heart of the death anxiety rooted in a nuclear age. President Kennedy himself had conceded in one speech, "A simple clash could escalate overnight into a holocaust of mushroom clouds."[21] Americans lived under a pervasive fear that nuclear war—purposeful or accidental—could produce sudden mass death. Kennedy's sudden and violent death was all too comprehensible in ways that the mass death of countless millions could not be.

This death anxiety surfaced in mass media. Along with newspapers, there were many examples of this in television shows and in movies. During the 1964 presidential election, the *Daily News* illustrated this. A November 27 editorial expressed concern about a transition of power in the wake of President Kennedy's assassination and its implications in a nuclear age.[22] On December 6, another editorial, titled "Assassination Problems Different Now," highlighted the potential for a mistake—or simple confusion—to result in a nuclear war: "There were no intercontinental ballistic missiles in Lincoln's day (following his assassination). At that time the nation could not be in immediate danger if someone were not found within a matter of minutes to become president and commander-in-chief." The editorial then added, "Now a few moments—the time between the start of an enemy nuclear attack and the order to make a nuclear counter-attack—could mean the difference between annihilation and some survival if not victory." Emphasizing the real possibility of mass death, it concluded that "such a foe might think in terms of assassination, not of the president alone, but [of] those in the immediate line of succession: the vice president and the two congressional leaders. It isn't hard to imagine the dismay and confusion after four such assassinations if they all occurred within a few minutes. The telephone lines would be a mess. And how could anyone be sure who was dead and who was alive?"[23]

So adding to the fear about mass death was the equally disturbing factor of chaos and how it could precipitate a nuclear exchange. In any event, the fear of mass death was exacerbated—and made more visible—when President Kennedy unexpectedly died, evoking the possibility of the death of countless others. This brings us back to the *Daily News* coverage of the 1964 presidential election, less than a year after Kennedy's assassination. Woven throughout that coverage was the same apprehension concerning mass death. The fear only intensified when Communist China achieved nuclear capability. On October 17, 1964, only a few weeks before the election, we find a front-page article in the *Daily News* titled "China's Bomb Widens U.S. Defense Role." It noted, "A world coexisting uneasily between two nuclear power blocs is now confronted with three."[24]

Ironically, the sudden death of yet another Kennedy, Robert, replicated the public's reaction of 1963, albeit in some different yet familiar terms, in 1968.

The Assassination of Senator Robert F. Kennedy

Not long after midnight on June 5, 1968, Senator Robert F. Kennedy— brother of the late president, former U.S. attorney general and member of the U.S. Senate between 1964 and 1968—was shot after giving a victory speech in Los Angeles, California. He had emerged victorious in the California Democratic primary election. Taken to Good Samaritan Hospital after suffering the attack at the Ambassador Hotel, he died from his wounds about twenty-six hours later. His body was flown to New York City. After a public viewing of a closed casket for two days, he was buried, like President Kennedy, at Arlington National Cemetery.

The public's perception of his death bore a striking similarity to that of his brother's. The role played by the media, the sense of a common experience producing a momentary halt in daily life, the image of youthful purpose halted by death and a death anxiety anchored in the fear over mass annihilation all were apparent in the reactions to Senator Kennedy's assassination. These developments all reared their heads in June 1968. While all of this appeared nationally, our concern here remains Genesee County. Accordingly, let us turn initially to the role played by county media in the wake of Senator Kennedy's murder and the related events it spawned.

For a week after the assassination, the three major networks—NBC, ABC, and CBS—devoted a total of 140 hours to the assassination and related events, such as Senator Kennedy's funeral, while eschewing commercials and regular programming. Such a focus was evident in Genesee County, as such newspapers as the *Daily News* devoted much of their space to the coverage of the Los Angeles event. Virtually the entire front page of the June 5 issue focused on Robert Kennedy's shooting—a full day before his actual death. Between the different types of media, print and otherwise, we witness once again the creation of a shared experience. However, the sense of a shared experience prompted by such extensive media coverage was even more intense in the reaction to Senator Kennedy's murder. Once again, the media covered the somber quality of Robert Kennedy's funeral while interjecting images of a young and purposeful Senator Kennedy. In effect, the public was reliving the assassination and burial of President Kennedy via the sudden death of his younger brother. On that June 5, under the headline "Whole Country Sick, Wounding of RFK Shocks Area Residents," the *Daily News* reported, "'It seemed like a recounting of the assassination of President Kennedy…' 'I cried…I couldn't believe it.' 'The whole country must be sick!' These were a few of the reactions of people on Main St. today as they talked of the wounding of US Sen. Robert F. Kennedy in California. Some said it signaled the need for an assessment of moral values by the people of the United States." It continued, "Clerks and downtown employees either had transistor radios tuned to reports, or would ask customers about the latest news. In stores handling television sets, all were on and many people were stopping periodically to check the reports and listening closely to programs."[25]

Remember that this reaction to the Kennedy shooting, and the shared experience of this event, is *before* reports of his actual death a day later. As one would expect, the front page of the June 6 issue was almost exclusively concerned with Senator Kennedy's death. "County Area Shares Grief in Tragedy," one headline exclaimed. It reported, "Genesee County joined the state and the nation today in paying tribute to the memory of Senator Robert F. Kennedy, who succumbed this morning after being fatally wounded by an assassin in Los Angeles." It continued, "The Kennedy Headquarters at Jackson and School Sts.…was also closed. Francis M. Repicci, who had been heading the Kennedy effort in this area, was shaken by the Senator's death." Repicci was quoted saying, "We have gone through this before, in 1963."[26]

As with President Kennedy's assassination, this shared experience induced a virtual halt to daily activities. One of Senator Kennedy's rivals for the Democratic nomination, Senator Eugene McCarthy, announced a suspension of campaigning for an indefinite period. In a June 6 article in the *Daily News*, readers learned that "Former LeRoy Supervisor Robert G. Fussell, who had been heading the McCarthy efforts in the County, said that he has been advised of the decision by the Senator's national headquarters to suspend all campaign efforts indefinitely."[27]

Along with such halts in daily life, the same Americans experienced again, five years later, the shock over an unexpected and violent death. A long article in the June 5 issue of the *Daily News* captured this sense of shock and outrage. "Genesee County Judge Glenn R. Morton termed it a 'stupid and senseless' act and said it was an indication of the 'tenor of our times.'" The same article quoted Chief of Police Stanley N. Smith, who was also "concerned over the overtones of lawlessness," saying, "First we had John F. Kennedy, then Martin Luther King and now, Sen. Kennedy. If we continue to tolerate [these] problems, the rioting at colleges and universities, we can look forward to more attacks and assaults on public officials." Finally, the police captain of LeRoy, Salvatore A. Falcone, said that this "awful tragedy…should awaken people to the fact that something must be done in the control of guns."[28]

Sentiments such as these produced, once again, a vivid contrast between the image of youthful energy and purpose alongside the reality of sudden death. In addition to the emotions produced by this second violent murder of a Kennedy in the span of only a few years, there was the perception among many that some of Robert Kennedy's youthfulness was found in the way he always seemed to be growing. In the 1950s, even before he became attorney general and his brother became president, he had a reputation for ruthlessness that was applied equally to suspected communists and labor leaders such as Jimmy Hoffa. In fact, it was an open secret even after becoming attorney general that he had little interest in civil liberties, as evidenced by such moves as allowing the Federal Bureau of Investigation to tap Martin Luther King Jr.'s telephone.

But after his brother's death—coupled with the deepening quagmire of Vietnam and worsening race relations in the United States—he showed a propensity for growth, a hallmark of a younger person changing as a consequence of seeing the world differently over time. He wasn't rigid, and it was this acceptance of change that allowed many to see him as young. The fact that he was only forty-two when he died only drove home the reality of his relative youth.

The perception that he was still growing—that he was young—stood in stark opposition to his unexpected death. The seriousness with which he approached the electorate, combined with a discernible open-mindedness, was captured in still another article in the same June 5 edition of the *Daily News*. Robert Kennedy, it said, "was, on the stump, intensive, hard-hitting and frequently very funny, especially in a self-deprecating way that might tend to undermine his alleged ruthlessness."[29]

A youthful Robert Kennedy's death embodied—even for many of his political opponents—a loss of hope for a renewal of an America torn apart by racial conflict, political division, war, and recurring assassinations. This same lack of hope for a predictable future goes to the heart of a death anxiety born of the nuclear age. How can one look optimistically to the future when at any moment millions could suddenly meet their end under a mushroom cloud? As we saw in the assassination of President Kennedy, the senseless death of millions remained incomprehensible. Reducing that vulnerability to one person is more understandable. Robert Kennedy understood this not as morbidity but as realism. The *Daily News* captured this side of Senator Kennedy's outlook: "Invariably, he [Robert Kennedy] would bounce down the steps of his campaign plane and, with little protection, plunge into frenzied, screaming crowds seeking to grab and tug at him. And inevitably we thought of Dallas and thought that this Kennedy was moving among strangers with much less protection than his brother did on that dark November day in 1963." Kennedy had moved among crowds, the article added, "with a certain sense of fatalism." It noted that in the midst of "the lulls in the campaign, at the end of a long day…we [reporters] often noticed as he rested and finally was alone, a look of infinite sadness, of terrible hurt. Most reporters noticed this and among those who knew him well, newsmen and staff aids, there was common agreement that that look wasn't there before November 22, 1963."[30]

Senator Kennedy had persisted in his quest to offer solutions to the problems confronting America in 1968, despite the looming threat of a nuclear holocaust. Like so many other Americans who knew that at any moment life could be drastically altered, he worked within a context of possible mass death that sobered his otherwise optimistic outlook for the future. He once remarked that he could not "be sitting around here calculating whether something I do is going to hurt my political situation in 1972….Who knows whether I'm going to be alive in 1972?"[31] It was known that his favorite poem was "I Have a Rendezvous with Death," by Alan Seeger, in which the narrator goes off to war thinking that it was worth the effort but expecting to die nevertheless.[32] Ironically, this was eventually the perspective of Martin Luther King Jr. by the end of his life.

THE ASSASSINATION OF
DR. MARTIN LUTHER KING JR.

In 1968, there was yet a third assassination that people in Genesee County responded to. This took place a little more than two months prior to that of Senator Kennedy. This was the murder of Dr. Martin Luther King Jr. on April 4. He, too, was shot, in this case as he stood on the balcony of a motel in Memphis, Tennessee. He was in the city to assist with a sanitation workers' strike, part of a Poor People's Campaign designed, as King's fellow civil rights leader Ralph Abernathy put it at the time, to "dramatize the plight of America's poor of all races and make very clear that they are sick and tired of waiting for a better life."[33] Ironically, in the midst of his campaign for the presidential nomination in Indianapolis only two months before his own death, Senator Kennedy learned of King's assassination. Despite warnings that the African American audience he was about to speak to could be furious, and without extensive bodyguard protection, Senator Kennedy took to the stage, where he echoed King's vision even as violent reactions to the civil rights leader's assassination were in progress elsewhere:

> *For those of you who are black and are tempted to be filled with hatred and distrust at the injustice of such an act, against all white people, I can only say that I feel in my own heart the same kind of feeling. I had a member of my family killed, but he was killed by a white man. But we have to make an effort in the United States, we have to make an effort to understand, to go beyond these rather difficult times.*[34]

This speech was credited with preserving the peace in Indianapolis in the wake of King's death. Nonetheless, illustrating the role played by a media capable of disseminating news rapidly and creating a common experience within a short time, the *Daily News* reported on April 5 that civil disturbances had erupted in numerous cities, including New York City; Tallahassee, Florida; Ita Benna, Mississippi; Boston; Jackson, Mississippi; Raleigh, North Carolina; and Detroit.[35] In the days that followed, this same newspaper reported additional civil disturbances, all of which constituted a key element in a shared experience largely fashioned by the media. "Racial Violence Leaves 16 Dead; Dawn Brings Calm," proclaimed one front-page headline. Another article exclaimed, "Chicago Wracked by Night-Long Siege of Terror."[36]

Despite President Lyndon Johnson's call for calm, reminding Genesee County and the country at large of Dr. King's advocacy of nonviolent solutions to America's ills, about 168 cities and towns endured violence.[37] Thirty-four thousand National Guardsmen and twenty-one thousand federal troops mobilized to restore order, making up what became the largest military deployment in modern times for a civil emergency.[38] Accordingly, the *Daily News*, in an April 6 editorial, commented that it "will be a long, long time before the nation recovers from the murder of Dr. Martin Luther King, Jr." The paper emphasized the shock accompanying King's unexpected death: "His slaying in Memphis, Tenn., had a shocking, staggering impact on the nation. It reverberated disbelief and disgust everywhere that such a thing could happen."[39]

As in the other two assassinations, the common experience of shock, accelerated by media reports, translated into a virtual halt in daily activities. On April 8, the *Daily News* reported that area schools would largely resume the following day. But even then, "special services and tributes will be paid in the schools in memory of Dr. Martin Luther King, Jr. on the day of his funeral."[40] An April 9 article titled "Nation Respectful in Tribute to Dr. King" spoke of numerous halts in daily activities, such as a bank holiday in New York.[41] In this same issue, an article echoing King's Poor People's Campaign appeared, titled "Low-Income Housing Termed Moral Duty by City Businessman." Readers were informed that the "City of Batavia and its City Council have a 'moral responsibility' to move quickly in getting public housing approved, the manager of a city concern said Monday night."[42]

The advocacy of such programs in Batavia illustrated the influence of King. So did the publication in the *Daily News* on April 9 of an editorial cartoon that depicted Mahatma Gandhi talking to King, with the caption underneath that read, "The odd thing about assassins, Dr. King, is that they think they've killed you."[43]

While a legacy of trying to enact King's beliefs is certainly part of a common experience, so, too, is a more sinister halt to daily routine—that of civil unrest. It should be remembered, however, that despite upheavals throughout the country, Genesee County remained peaceful. Unlike Rochester in neighboring Monroe County, which had experienced racial unrest only four years before, in 1964, Genesee County's tiny African American population, amounting to no more than 3 percent of the county population, did not respond to King's murder with civil unrest. Unlike a city such as Rochester, Genesee County did not feature an African American perception of a hostile police force exhibiting racism toward an African

American minority. Indeed, the reaction to King's death produced numerous responses in schools and the business community emphasizing that the death of King was a loss to the community at large, African American and white. As late as five days after Dr. King's assassination, the *Daily News* ran a front-page story that reported civil disturbances in reaction to King's death in Baltimore; Cincinnati; Wilmington, Delaware; Youngstown, Ohio; Pittsburgh; and Washington, D.C.[44] Even shopping for Easter came to a pronounced halt, as the *Daily News* reported on April 10. Underneath the headline "Riots Disrupt Easter in Some Sectors," readers learned that "several surveys have shown that consumers—even though not immediately endangered—turn cautious, postpone sales and take a wait-and-see attitude when trouble abounds."[45] Despite national upheavals and cautious consumers, Genesee County remained calm.

While a common experience accelerated by modern mass media took *unique* forms in the wake of King's death, another aspect of the county's reaction to his assassination did not. As in the other two killings, the imagery of youthful energy and purpose stood in clear opposition to sudden death.

This image of purpose and idealism translated into King's commitment toward those without political power or economic privilege, regardless of race. An unwillingness to accept the status quo is a hallmark of youthful

The relative lack of racial tensions in the county was long-standing. An example of this is a photograph of an integrated school in Batavia from 1894. This photograph is from the Ross Street School.

thinking, regardless of actual age. The fact that King was only thirty-nine when he died only served to accentuate this image of youthful purpose. The perception of King as a young person filled with a passionate belief that the world could be improved emerged at a moment in time when many of the baby boom generation thought in similar terms. Accordingly, their youthful idealism became inextricably bound with his. King's stand against the Vietnam War intensified this synthesis between young people and King. As he stated in one speech, "I refuse to accept the view that mankind is so tragically bound to the starless midnight of racism and war that the bright daybreak of peace and brotherhood can never become a reality....I believe that unarmed truth and unconditional love will have the final word."[46]

The *Daily News* captured these sentiments in its depictions of King. On April 5, an editorial titled "Even If They Kill Us, We Still Have Power" insisted that King's belief in the capacity of people to change the world for the better was one that was not only possible but also attainable through nonviolence: "In Albany, Ga., in 1962, when Negro crowds hurled bottles and bricks at policemen, King suspended his marches and called a day of penance, going through the poolrooms collecting knives and other weapons. 'We cannot win this struggle with bottles and bricks,' he said."[47]

Not all agreed with King's endorsement of nonviolence as a means for addressing America's ills, especially those of race. The dissent of Malcolm X and his followers was an example of this. Many who expressed sympathy for King's movement held an optimistic belief that change was possible without violence and hatred and that it could operate within the broad structure of American institutions, despite their flaws. This view stressed a rejuvenation of basic American beliefs that were present from the beginning but lost over time.

However, King's sudden and violent death weakened that optimism for many Americans. It stood in stark contrast to the youthful idealism characterizing King's outlook. It made even moderates despair over what seemed to be little more than a decade of assassinations. Coupled with a war without fronts or clear objectives, it drove home the vulnerability of the individual in a world teetering on the edge of nuclear annihilation. When Senator Kennedy, a year before his death, took to the Senate floor to state his opposition to the Johnson administration's bombing in Vietnam, concluding that "we are all participants" and that "we must also feel as men the anguish of what it is we are doing," he was echoing King with respect to the direction that America was going.[48] The *Daily News* articulated a similar concern. All Americans—as illustrated by assassinations, violence in America's streets and a war without clear objectives consuming America's youth—remained vulnerable. Their lives could end suddenly and senselessly. For instance, an April 25, 1968, article headlined "Air Force, Civilian Views Differ on Bomb Defenses" reported, "Air Force and civilian analysts differ sharply in a Pentagon intelligence dispute already casting a shadow over U.S. plans to defend against Soviet bombers of the 1970s." The article, emphasizing the real possibility of nuclear war, goes on: "Basically at issue is the soundness of a national-level assessment that the Soviets will not develop a supersonic strategic bomber with far-reaching missiles during the next six years. Gen. John P. McConnell, Air Force Chief of Staff, thinks they will and argues the United States should build some new 2,000 miles-per-hour interceptors able to shoot them down." In conclusion, "The four-star general said he felt the Soviets would indeed put into operation a new supersonic bomber capable of 'delivering an extremely long-range, high-speed air-to-ground missile' against the United States by 1976."[49]

Even at the height of a shooting war in Vietnam, with the pages of the *Daily News* replete with news of county youth entering military service, serving in Vietnam and sometimes being wounded or killed there, there was attention paid to the larger picture of—and anxiety over—nuclear war. While in some ways nuclear war remained a politically taboo subject, the pronounced fears it unleashed did not go away. While military and scientific personnel by 1968 were generally seen as helping the country defend itself against other nations, the prospect of mass death still reared its head time and again. Here we see the public's ambiguity about the nuclear establishment. It appeared necessary and yet was deeply distrusted. Part of that distrust was the reality of personal vulnerability, an exposure to sudden death that dramatically played out, once again, in the unexpected and violent death of King.

ALL THREE ASSASSINATIONS GENERATED an array of emotional responses, which included those discernible in Genesee County. In the interest of brevity, I have relied on a widely circulated newspaper in Genesee County between 1963 and 1968, the *Daily News*. A newspaper such as this expresses—and helps to shape—public opinion. Nonetheless, as that same newspaper depends on its readership for revenue, it can never get too far ahead of the public. Hence, it is an indication of how many people feel about the issues of the day—in this case, three pivotal assassinations in the 1960s.

Modern mass media—including the newspaper—stressed the reactions of the public to these murders. In the descriptions of reactions to these events, and in the narratives about the events themselves, a perception of a common experience appeared. Individuals identified with the emotional reactions of others locally and beyond. They found that many others were shocked by these events. They also learned that in neighboring communities that shock translated into a virtual halt in normal, daily activities.

Part of this shock was rooted in the sudden, violent deaths of leaders perceived as young—both chronologically and in terms of their purpose and idealism. The view that they were young—and struck down in the prime of life—only served to contrast their active, meaningful lives with the finality of death. Such an understanding worked to heighten a death anxiety already pronounced in American life after the explosion of the first atomic bombs in 1945. Many already felt vulnerable, despite the seeming assurances of prosperity, predictability, and hope for the future visible in American society. If the safety of prominent leaders remained uncertain, how could ordinary people feel certain? American life certainly went on, but it advanced with a tentative quality not giving in to what would otherwise be an unfettered American optimism. The question remaining is this: can there be an unlimited American optimism in the wake of these assassinations and the specter of a nuclear exchange? Only time and new circumstances will allow us to answer that question.

CHAPTER 2

BATAVIA EXPLODES

COLD WAR ANXIETY AND THE PREPAREDNESS DRILL OF 1956

In spite of living in a country that had a clear superiority by every metric, American citizens remained at high alert for an imminent invasion no Kremlin figure ever seriously contemplated.
—*Brian T. Brown,* Someone Is Out to Get Us

On Friday, September 14, 1956, a civil defense exercise commenced at Batavia's Veterans Administration Hospital.

At ten o'clock that morning, civil defense sirens blared, announcing a simulated fire raging in Ward D, part of a "disaster test" designed to re-create the conditions that would result from an explosion produced by an "enemy attack." A second simulation that day included a nuclear attack that resulted in the destruction of the Batavia Post Office building. During this second simulated attack, a postal truck carried emergency supplies and equipment to a relocation site reached via West Main Street and Redfield Parkway. A second postal truck supervised by the foreman of mails, Arthur Norton, transported more people and equipment over Jefferson Avenue, Washington Avenue, Ellicott Avenue, Richmond Avenue and Redfield Parkway. A third postal truck remained on standby, while the Veterans Hospital supply officer, John Lane, ordered one truck to facilitate removal from what was left of the post office building while simultaneously keeping eight additional vehicles on standby. Officials drew on the help of volunteers responding to sirens located throughout the county. In its Saturday

Front of the Veterans Hospital in Batavia, two years before the drill.

edition, the *Daily News* reported that the exercise was an unqualified success.[50] This drill serves as a stark reminder of the political and cultural realities of Cold War America in 1956—and the anxiety regarding the possibility of a nuclear confrontation with the Soviet Union apparent in the county.[51]

The events of September 14 are reducible to a mere narrative—the "fire" in Ward D broke out at 10:00 a.m., and within five minutes, three pieces of fire equipment arrived at the "disaster" scene, followed twenty minutes later by an additional eleven pieces of equipment. Such a narrative, while interesting, prompts the obvious question: Why did a "disaster" produced by the "enemy" take place at all? In addition, other questions arise. What was the nature of this "disaster," why was there a clear anxiety about its real possibility, who was this "enemy" and how could such an intrusion reach into the heart of an otherwise stable and peaceful Genesee County in 1956?

To answer these questions, I offer here what one scholar has referred to as "thick description"[52]—that is, a narrative detailing what happened while including a description of its social context. The only way to have a deeper

Earlier anxiety about war. Genesee County men leaving for World War I. They are seated in front of the county courthouse.

understanding of why the feigned disaster was happening at all is to situate it within the wider context of Cold War America—and Cold War Genesee County—in 1956.

WHAT HAPPENED—AND WHY

To appreciate the events of September 14, 1956, in Batavia, one has to place them squarely within the Cold War moment of the time. In chronological terms, the Cold War encompassed a broader period. Historians generally agree that the Cold War began at the end of World War II in 1945 and lasted until the collapse of the Soviet Union in 1991. This conflict between the communist and the noncommunist world displayed five characteristics, all of which appeared in Batavia in September 1956. The first of these is what outgoing president Dwight D. Eisenhower called the "military-industrial complex."[53] In this 1961 speech to the nation, Eisenhower warned of the "unwarranted influence, whether sought or unsought, by the military-industrial complex." He added a warning: "We must never let the weight of this combination endanger our liberties or democratic processes."[54] As scholars have long pointed out, the maintenance of such a setting required the perpetuation of an atmosphere of ceaseless crisis—a social environment evident in the Batavia Veterans Administration Hospital drill.

A second feature of the Cold War discernible in this drill is the necessity of a popular culture facilitating the militarization of a society—that is, one in which permanent arms escalation makes sense. This was the era of Mickey Spillane stories about the killing of communists associated with the chief Cold War rival, the Union of Soviet Socialist Republics; comic strips featuring Captain America fighting to make America safe from Soviet enemies; and "duck and cover" exercises for children at school. When the hospital mandated employees to view the film *One Plane, One Bomb, One City* in the week leading up to the drill, the hospital was simply participating in what had become, by 1956, standard cultural fare in Cold War America.[55]

The cultural preoccupation with a communist threat remained as apparent in Genesee County as it was in the nation at large. Local media continuously stressed the lethal quality of communist threats, subversion, and attacks. Newspaper articles emphasized the necessity of American involvement in the Korean War, as evidenced by the participation of county residents in a conflict half a world away. "Airman from Oakfield Expects Duty in Korea," proclaimed Batavia's *Daily News* in 1953.[56] A soldier from Corfu served in the Third Infantry Division in Korea, while soldiers from Bergen and LeRoy served with the Twenty-Fourth Infantry Division there.[57] There were constant reminders of how *hot* the *Cold* War was capable of becoming and of how tragic the consequences were for some county families.

For example, an article in the fall of 1953 in the *Daily News* reported the return of the remains of a young soldier to Genesee County from Korea. Private John V. Peca of LeRoy was twenty-four years old and left behind a wife, brother, and parents.[58] Such stories abounded in the earlier years of the Cold War, as the fighting raged in Korea. Other accounts revealed that soldiers initially listed as missing in action subsequently reappeared as killed in action, such as eighteen-year-old Army Corporal Norman F. Smart of Batavia. His brother, Private First Class Robert D. Smart, was also in Korea. While there, he suffered wounds.[59]

Those from the county not killed or wounded sometimes languished as prisoners of war in communist prison camps. This, too, brought home to rural Genesee County residents the nation's very real conflict with the communist world. Army sergeant James D. Dewey initially survived a prisoner of war camp only to succumb to malnutrition while in communist hands.[60] Some county residents who survived communist prison camps spoke of Russian involvement in the functioning of those camps in North Korea. One of these was U.S. Air Force captain William N. Preston of Batavia. He endured two and a half years as a prisoner in North Korea. He spoke of "many high-ranking Russians [who] visited a North Korean camp where the Reds were trying to wrest 'confessions' and information from captured Americans by starvation and other maltreatment."[61]

The many media accounts of those killed, wounded, and mistreated by communists during a very hot Cold War period reminded readers of the threat posed by the communist world. Preston spoke before groups about an imminent threat to democracy in need of recognition. Once recognized, this threat had to be fought. He was quoted in one newspaper article saying, "The only solution to the problem of world communism…is to 'chop it off wherever it breaks out.'"[62]

Preston's call for a containment of communism appeared in other county publications. In the early summer of 1953, the *Daily News* invoked the memory of county residents who lost their lives in the necessary struggle against "an insidious doctrine in a far-off land."[63] The aggressiveness of this "insidious doctrine" required America—indeed, Genesee County—to remain vigilant. Therefore, even when the Korean War ended with an armistice on July 27, 1953, talk continued about the necessity of drills and other acts of preparedness—such as the one three years later at the Veterans Administration Hospital. Nonetheless, that drill was only one in a series of preparedness events. Four months after the armistice, the Batavia School District commenced bomb shelter drills. One county media outlet reported, "Compliance by Batavia Schools with State Civil Defense instructions for bomb shelter drills is not to be considered an unnecessary or hysteria situation. As everyone knows, the threat of attack on the United States is no myth."[64]

A little over a week later, that same publication alerted county residents to "atom bomb drills." This announcement outlined the procedures involved: "Principals will devise warning signals to be different from the fire drill bells. When the alert is given, students will walk to a designated place in each school, sit down and put their heads between their knees and also protect the backs of their necks with coats or their hands."[65] Three years before the drill, another hospital in Genesee County practiced for the near certainty of a Soviet attack. St. Jerome Hospital conducted preparations "for [a] possible war catastrophe." Along with a photograph of two nurses demonstrating care for a "victim" that is actually a model dummy, this article described hospital protocol at St. Jerome in the event of an attack: "A special alert signal has been chosen which, when heard over the loud speaker system, will not alarm patients. Control groups and receiving points have been designated. Special rooms have been assigned from which furniture would be quickly moved and cots placed. Trained groups will be in readiness at the sound of the alert to carry out the plan."[66]

The discussion of preparedness intensified the militarization of county culture, one in which permanent arms escalation seemed appropriate. Added to this was the cultural emphasis on the communist threat evident in movies routinely shown in Genesee County alongside public lectures concerning dangers emanating from the Kremlin. Some county residents argued that homegrown communists also posed a danger. These domestic communists had no direct link with the Kremlin. In one letter to the editor, signed by a "Batavian," readers read a defense of Senator Joseph McCarthy. This letter included the view that "communism is our worst enemy. All the Communists aren't in North Korea."[67] Letters such as this one appeared alongside photographs of a Bergen mother celebrating her twenty-two-year-old son's release from a prisoner of war camp and an article reassuring readers that television star Lucille Ball was not a communist.[68] The threat even arose in some churches, as one article pointed out. Readers learned that "thousands of clergymen adopted the Communist slogan 'Bring the Boys Home,' and so helped speed U.S. demobilization after World War II."[69] Articles such as this joined with editorials pointing to "communists in America who craftily play their game of subversion and espionage" and advertisements for anticommunist films such as *I Married a Communist* and *I Was a Communist for the F.B.I.*[70] All of this combined with consistent recognition of Genesee County's loss of service members during the Korean War to produce an understandable Cold War anxiety concerning communist threats.[71]

This brings us to a third Cold War motif illustrated in the Batavia drill. Here we discover the misconception that there are ways for people to protect themselves against the effects of a nuclear blast. Analysts such as Herman Kahn, in his book *On Thermonuclear War*, contended that it was possible to undertake a nuclear war without producing total destruction.[72] Henry Kissinger subsequently made the same point. He asserted that a nuclear war does not have to be as destructive as many assumed it would be.[73] Therefore, the Batavia drill featured actions designed to reassure the public in a psychological sense but which, in a scientific sense, were meaningless. Post-explosion radiological surveys designed to offer areas for medical treatment of victims near ground zero, temporary aid stations at the John

Kennedy School, neatly organized medical supply stations, and dispatchers at the Batavia Fire Headquarters sending equipment to the Veterans Administration Hospital are all examples of efforts to deny the devastating consequences of an atomic blast.[74]

Here we arrive at a fourth theme discernible in the drill: the atmosphere resulting from American involvement in international affairs during the Cold War. The Cold War produced a peacetime army taking the place of token American forces traditionally maintained since 1783. Joined with the newly created Central Intelligence Agency, the National Security Council, and RAND (research and development) Corporation, this peacetime army—with a peacetime draft—normalized the sense of urgency and danger characterizing the Cold War.

The draft in Genesee County throughout the 1950s, before, during, and after the Korean War, was a prominent story in county media. The draft was a central part of reality for young men during this period, a reality not easily ignored. "Leave for Military Duty" was the caption to a newspaper photograph showing three young men who "comprised today's Selective Service contingent leaving for service in the armed forces." Emphasizing to the reader the necessity of military preparedness, the caption ended with a somber reminder. "The Draft Board office," readers learned, "announced next month's call will be for six on Nov. 13."[75] Along with a continuous stream of draftees necessary even in "peacetime" to counter the communist threat, there were also large charts outlining the military options available to young men in the county.

In the late summer of 1956, a half-page announcement in the *Daily News* addressed to "Genesee County Young Men" contained a detailed chart outlining "how you may choose to discharge your military obligation." The chart distinguished "Regular Service" from "The Reserve Program." Within each category, age requirements correlated with the branch of service and the attendant length of service required in each. Underneath, readers discovered the names and addresses of recruiters for each branch of service. There was also a list of names of civilian members of the county's "Armed Services Advisory Committee." Adding to the projection of community support in the effort to remain vigilant was the note that twenty local businesses, ranging from a paint store to a contractor through a tire store, had, "in the interest of community betterment," sponsored "the space for the message above."[76]

The previous page of that same issue offered another reminder of the widespread presence of the Cold War in Genesee County. Readers discovered that "most county doctors aid in civil defense." The civil defense director, M.O. Clement, reported that about 75 percent of the fifty or so physicians in Genesee County belonged to the county chapter of the national Civil Defense program. What was their purpose? As residents learned, the "purpose of the registration is so that the doctors will be available in time of any emergency."[77] In this environment of militarization, anxiety, and perceived foreign threat, it should not surprise us that army weapons carriers and ambulances transporting "blast victims" were seen in the streets of Batavia during the VA hospital drill.

This permanent state of war is indicative of a fifth Cold War theme apparent in the drill. The Cold War was not simply a traditional conflict between great powers. It was instead an ideological clash between two social systems—authoritarian communism and a republican, capitalist society. This ideological aspect manifested itself during the drill and the week leading up to it. For example, Veterans Administration chaplains spoke of the drill's significance in this respect in services conducted on Sunday, September 9. The coordinating committee of the drill included Catholic nuns.[78] Because direct, full-scale conflict was not a realistic option in a nuclear age, much of the Cold War—when not being fought through smaller nations—was conducted on the terrain of ideas. Chief among these ideas was the notion of the freedom of individual conscience. Hence the symbolic involvement of the chaplains and the nuns, demonstrating that America remained a free society in which individuals could practice their religion without governmental interference. This contrasted sharply with the official atheism of the Soviet Union and other communist societies. The Batavia drill was a civil exercise in the demonstrated superiority of American-style democracy. Therefore, the need to contain an evil communist system was an effort evident in many small towns around the country in 1956—and Batavia was not an exception.

THE DRILL

According to the VA hospital's "Observers Report—Disaster Exercise," the drill began at 10:00 a.m. A simulated fire, produced by a theoretical explosion, induced chaos. On Ward D, Charles S. Livingston, a Veterans Administration physician and the hospital's manager, called on the civil defense disaster coordinator to seek assistance from the civil defense forces. Assistance also came from the Genesee County Mutual Fire System.

Events then moved quickly. Several minutes later, firefighting equipment arrived at the hospital. The New York State civil defense director, General C.R. Huebner, was notified that a "disaster" had taken place. Clement told him that fifty Batavians had been "hurt." Situation reports were then relayed to Huebner, keeping the general informed and requesting that the state send needed medical supplies. The New York State Civil Defense Commission provided one hundred units of medicines, 150 litter cots, blankets, dressings, and medical supplies. The American Red Cross and the Salvation Army subsequently orchestrated blood supplies and canteen work, respectively. Blood supplies were flown in from Buffalo, and transportation and police escorts were organized. By 11:06 a.m., Huebner had notified Clement that four hundred doses of sedatives were being flown in from Olean, New York. By 11:08 a.m., Clement had told Huebner that the "crisis" was under control and that additional assistance was not needed. Subsequent to the activation of civil defense sirens, twelve Genesee County fire departments dispatched units to Batavia to help with the "disaster." Throughout the day, civil defense auxiliary police worked to guard the entrances to the hospital. They also worked to keep all streets leading to the hospital clear.

Fire departments used water from the artificial lake located on the Veterans Administration grounds to control the "fire." The "fire" was brought under control in about half an hour. Despite the "explosion" and "fire," the water supply in the hospital remained functional. "Casualties" were lying in the hospital hallways, where there was a quick distribution of medicines and blood. In a federal government memorandum dated September 17, 1956, it was concluded that the drill, designed to simulate the "reality" of an atomic blast, revealed "efficient planning and organization" and "relative quiet in the evacuation process."[79]

The drill and the official appraisals of it depict a nuclear attack as one in which those injured and sick received reassuring and efficient medical attention. Government personnel tended to those sick from radioactive poisoning. Indeed, the assumption that there would be medical and governmental personnel in place *after* the attack remained unquestioned.

ANALYSIS

The drill reveals an America, and a county, in which a permanent crisis is a natural part of life. In 1956, a culture of fear and anxiety enveloped American life, and Batavia was no exception. As the *State of New York Operational Survival*

Plan reminds us, drills such as this one were part of a "Plan for Survival" that was a necessary response to a condition of permanent war.[80] However, fear alone could be paralyzing. As a result, it was necessary to cultivate a sense of optimism. Therefore, there was a national and local effort to convince people that a nuclear attack was not necessarily fatal.

Hence, it is not surprising that the drill so confidently depicted available water supplies, medicines, and medical personnel capable of caring for the wounded. This meant the rational and efficient organization of air and land transport routes, along with fully functioning utilities even amid the chaos of a nuclear blast. In effect, Batavia served—as countless other towns did around the country in the 1950s—as a giant air raid shelter in which the public could indeed survive a nuclear blast, and comfortably so.

The permanent war society exuded clarity. This was a titanic struggle between good and evil in which there could be no room for doubt about the possibility of survival. Nowhere in such drills could realities such as 1,500 Hiroshima-size atomic bombs in the American arsenal alone by 1962—in other words, ten tons of TNT for every man, woman, and child on earth—be acknowledged. The inherent uncertainties of a nuclear attack preclude the possibility of assumptions built into the Batavia drill. The thrust of the drill was a civil defense predicated on evacuation and sheltering. In an actual attack, this would have proved futile. For example, an enemy intent on attacking a population could just as easily retarget populations fleeing or being transported to other areas. Even if populations could be transported, it would not ultimately matter, as protection against the blast, intense radiation, heat, and mass fires would render evacuation—and medical care—useless. The drill embodied—as did similar drills around the United States throughout the 1950s—the idea that life can be lived indefinitely on top of a pile of nuclear weapons. Not wanting to face what that meant in the event of a nuclear exchange, Americans in the 1950s—including those in the Batavian drill—encouraged a view of the nuclear world denying the obvious.[81] The point of these public exercises was to accustom people to the routine denial of imminent danger. In effect, people tiptoed around the peril without really acknowledging the nature of the actual crisis—the distinct possibility of an atomic explosion capable of wielding a mortal blow to human survival itself. Instead, all that remained was the purported moral legitimacy of the struggle between the United States and the USSR, as well as the belief that, if need be, a nuclear war could be won and that there would be survivors in a recognizable world, capable of carrying on even in a post-blast age.

IN SO MANY WAYS—AND despite the popular imagery of *Happy Days*, *Laverne and Shirley*, and *Grease*—America in the 1950s was uncertain, anxious, and, in some ways, adrift. Frustration over the inability to confront militarily the Soviet communist system amounted to a frustration with modern life itself—the same modern technology and science producing benefits also conjured up a world in which simpler notions of us or them, or right and wrong, could not be approached more directly. After all, there was always the specter of nuclear war lurking in the background.

As a result, a fantasy world took hold—worlds neat, tidy, and predictable *despite* the possibility of nuclear annihilation. The possibility of an atomic blast remained anchored in a view of the world in which America's permanent post–World War II mission was to convey an image of the United States as one in which Americans defend liberty—at all costs—even in a nuclear age. That defense could translate into victory, even in a world living in the shadow of a mushroom cloud. All of this, despite the ironic comment of Eisenhower in 1953, that the United States and the Soviet Union must address the grim world created by the Cold War, one where there is "not a way of life at all, in any true sense…under a cloud of war, it was humanity hanging from a cross of iron."[82] Despite such concerns, the belief in the possibility of actually winning a nuclear war persisted. Viewing the world as so many did in the 1950s contained unfortunate consequences later on, as the division of the world into "us" and "them" paved the way into the quagmires of wars around the world, which takes us beyond the scope of this chapter. In the end, the most ironic development of all was the eventual triumph of American freedom over the darkness of Soviet tyranny. Amazingly, this happened without nuclear war. One can only hope that such good fortune will continue into the near future.

CHAPTER 3

IMMIGRANTS TO WHITE ETHNICS

Migration is a fundamental human activity.
—*Roger Daniels,* Coming to America

In the nineteenth and early twentieth centuries, two groups of immigrants arrived in Genesee County. While they were not the only new arrivals, the experiences of the Irish and the Italians embodied many of the realities of other groups smaller in numbers, such as the Germans, Poles, Greeks, and Chinese.[83] The first immigrant groups arriving in the county were the English and the Scots, who moved to the county largely from Pennsylvania and New England.[84] The focus in this chapter on the Irish and the Italians is due to both their relatively large numbers when compared to the other European and Asian groups and their different cultures as compared to the English and the Scots. They eventually assimilated into the dominant American culture and its myriad institutions. Here one can differentiate between *English* and *Scotch* on the one hand and *American* on the other. By the time of Irish and Italian arrival in Genesee County, what had once been English or Scottish culture had developed into what can be understood as an American nationality. That nationality developed as an expression of English and Scottish culture that was a variety of English/Scottish language and culture that was understood by immigrants as American. It was to that variant of English/Scottish culture that first the Irish, and then the Italians, were expected to assimilate to in Genesee County.[85]

RES. OF GEORGE RUPPRECHT, MAYOR,
COR OF ELLICOT & EVANS STS., BATAVIA, NEW YORK.

Home of the native-born county elite during the time of Irish and Italian immigration to Batavia in the nineteenth century.

Accordingly, this chapter contains two sections, one on the Irish and the other on the Italians. We will turn first to the Irish, who initially arrived in large numbers in the early nineteenth century, meeting the need for labor in the construction of the Erie Canal. A different mode of transportation—the railroad—brought Italian immigrants. In their case, they largely worked on those railroads by the early 1880s.[86]

THE IRISH

In the spring of 1849, a group of Irish immigrants in LeRoy greeted a Roman Catholic priest from Batavia, Father Edward Dillon. Dillon had traveled from Batavia to say Mass for the first time in LeRoy. Despite the absence of a Roman Catholic church in LeRoy, he conducted Mass in the "Round House," a public building on West Main Street. At the conclusion of the service, Dillon announced that he planned to journey to LeRoy one Sunday every month to say Mass. Dennis F. Butler volunteered the use of his residence on Pleasant Street for this monthly observance. Three months later, in July, Bishop John Timon arrived in LeRoy to offer support to the small but committed Irish congregation. By Christmas Eve 1849, that committed group of Irish Catholics had succeeded in building a small wooden church given the name of Saint Francis Church. A High Mass took place there on that Christmas Eve of 1849.[87]

At first glance, this appears to be the simple story of a group of Irish immigrants joining to build a church. But a deeper look at this event in LeRoy reveals a far greater significance, one going to the heart of the meaning of Catholicism for countless Irish immigrants and their descendants in Genesee County and, indeed, beyond. Discernible in this event is the intimate relationship between Irish Americans and Irish Catholic nationalism, on display in LeRoy but with roots in the Ireland these immigrants left behind.[88]

The relationship between Irish immigrants and the Roman Catholic Church differed dramatically from that of other Catholic immigrant groups. This is especially so when compared to the relationship between Italian immigrants from southern Italy and the Italian Catholic Church. The church in Ireland, along with its clergy and congregants, were outsiders in their own country. The Catholicism of Ireland remained outside of the upper levels of the Irish social structure, dominated by English Protestants. This latter domination, existing in various forms since the twelfth century, remained embodied in Henry VIII's assumption of the title "King of

Ireland" in 1541. English efforts from that moment on to solidify control in Ireland were never fully successful—even with the imposition of the "penal laws" in Ireland in the mid-seventeenth century. One scholar, Thomas Sowell, has written that these laws functioned to deprive "the Irish of many basic rights. Irish Catholics could neither vote nor be elected to public office, nor practice law, nor be a student or faculty member at a university. Irish Catholic children could not be educated legally, nor could Catholic churches function freely and openly, nor could Catholics own any significant property or exercise basic legal or political rights. The openly avowed purpose of these laws was to keep the Irish subjugated and impoverished." Sowell adds, "Catholic priests often went 'underground' to serve their parishioners; schools were secretly conducted, and vigilantes struck against those forcibly collecting tithes among Catholics to support Protestant churches, against landlords evicting tenants—or against indigenous Irish men collaborating with the enemy."[89]

The history of English colonial efforts in Ireland shaped the kind of Catholic consciousness in evidence in LeRoy in 1849. This tradition accompanied the Irish immigrants for whom a Roman Catholic Church in Genesee County meant so much. The legacy of a church with obvious political implications for a conquered people was, if anything, exacerbated by the Great Famine between 1845 and 1849. While there had been fourteen partial or complete potato famines in Ireland between 1816 and 1842, it was the arrival in the fall of 1845 of *Phytophthora infestans*—a rapidly spreading and uniquely unpredictable strain of fungus disease—that destroyed the dietary staple of Ireland's laboring poor.[90] Prevailing ideas about social responsibility, along with the English colonizers' disdain of the Irish, combined to prevent concerted governmental action to alleviate the suffering resulting from the shortage of a dietary staple among those least able to withstand economic upheaval. An article in Batavia's *Republican Advocate* in the spring of 1846 reported:

> *The intelligence from Ireland is painfully distressing. In some parts of Tippererara, the peasantry, unable any longer to resist the cravings of hunger, have taken the case in their own hands, plundered the provision shops, broken into the flour mills and helped themselves. The town of Clonmell is in a state of siege. Troops are obliged to escort provisions as they pass through the streets, and the unfortunate creatures whose bones are described as protruding through their skins, are kept down by the fear of the bayonet…*

Accounts pour in upon us daily of the increasing distress…In many places there are no potatoes left.…

Even at Turlough, in the immediate neighborhood of this town, many families are at this moment, we learn, without food.[91]

Under such horrific circumstances, desperate Irish laborers routinely looked to the church for material and spiritual help. Departure from Ireland did not mean departure from this close relationship between the church and the people. Arriving and largely settling in New York, Illinois, Massachusetts, and Pennsylvania, Irish immigrants maintained their strong Catholic identity and customs.

This was a Catholicism of a united priest and peasant. This tradition of resistance also manifested itself in Genesee County decades later, when Irish American Catholics generally refused to abandon their Catholicism in the face of threats from the Ku Klux Klan after World War I. Like the earlier priest and peasant, they stood in opposition to all that was Protestant. In Ireland, that resistance had also meant opposition to all that was English. To be Irish and Catholic—whether in Ireland or in Genesee County— meant to possess a complete identity forged in the crucible of English colonialism. Daniel O'Connor's Catholic Association, founded in 1823, is a prime example of the merging of Irish ethnicity and Catholicism. A movement funded by the "Catholic rent" of as little as a penny per month, it was an effort combining the concerns of tenants with the Catholic community as a whole. Its local agents were typically priests engaging in a daily process of political education about parliamentary debates and local matters. Irish populism and the agitation of the clergy merged openly in the association, a combination apparent in the United States as well. As an 1847 *Republican Advocate* article reveals, Genesee County was not an exception to this national trend. Under the headline "Relief for Ireland!" the paper reported:

Every paper which has been received for some days back, has contained accounts of the efforts made in all directions to extend aid to the starving and suffering millions of Ireland. New York, Albany, Utica, Syracuse, Rochester, Buffalo, and many of the smaller towns, have contributed largely, and the work appears to have just begun.

In LeRoy, on the evening of the meeting, $170 in cash, was collected.…

The cheerfulness with which the American citizens contribute of their substance to keep from starving the millions *who have been impoverished by* English legislation, *should serve as a check to their arrogance and self-complacency in the future.*[92]

While Genesee County in particular and the United States in general did not impose on Irish immigrants the trauma of the famine, it did nonetheless relegate the Irish immigrant generation to the position of maligned outsider. This pattern was repeated across the Atlantic. As the Irish moved into New York, they encountered a Protestant, British-American culture featuring values that stood in contrast to those of the Irish. Mid-nineteenth-century New York was a Protestant civilization stressing a workplace of artisanship and the ownership and development of farms. Impoverished Irish immigrants posed a threat to an economy still essentially preindustrial in nature, one featuring the medieval occupational hierarchy of master, journeyman, and apprentice—not to mention the Jeffersonian notion of the yeoman farmer. Desperately poor Irish immigrants, arriving in increasing numbers, offered little more than a willingness to work at any menial task. Not surprisingly, the growing number of unskilled laborers posed a challenge to those already employed in such tasks. This induced a disdain among American workers who viewed the presence of the Irish as a threat to both their wages and job security. Concerns over the presence of Irish toilers also extended beyond economic issues—witness an article in Batavia's *Spirit of the Times*, published in April 1852: "The Irish settlement up the Canal was yesterday the scene of another disgraceful row. The Galway men who have been assaulted on several occasions by the Mayo men, having their shanties torn down and burned, and their property destroyed, assembled in a large body determined to avenge their wrongs by a fearless retaliation. Having organized themselves, they proceeded to the homes of their antagonists, demolished their shanties and property without stint."[93]

Such accounts reflected a popular belief that Irish immigrants were a permanently dispossessed class unsuited to democratic America. They appeared to be an unruly and politically unpredictable class with religious ties to a Vatican itself perceived as inappropriate to democratic, Protestant America.[94] The Catholicism of the Irish American remained the root of the economic situation of the immigrant. Nativist writers often highlighted "Irish Catholic traits." These supposedly innate tendencies appeared in both the racial assumptions of the mid-nineteenth century and in the Catholicism of the Irish. This surfaced in popular culture, and from this perspective, it translated into the economic situation of the immigrant and

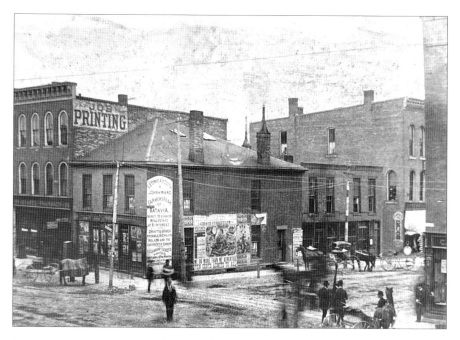

Downtown Batavia during the time of Irish immigration in the 1860s.

the generation born in the United States. These "characteristics" included the portrayal of the Irish as lacking the habits of thrift and self-denial necessary for success in a republican democracy. Instead, Irish Catholicism was viewed as undisciplined and fatalistic, qualities routinely connected to Catholicism. The prejudice against the Irish was also a prejudice against Roman Catholicism, and it was so prevalent in the United States in the 1800s that the *Republican Advocate*, in a manner rare in this historical moment, reminded its readers that Catholicism was indeed capable of inclusion in Protestant, democratic America. In the summer of 1849, an article pointedly sympathetic to Catholicism and implicitly so toward the Irish commented on the role played by nuns: "To witness the untiring zeal and devotion with which the Sisters of Charity give all their time to the care of the inmates of the Hospital without inquiring after their religious creeds, will banish from any mind all the prejudices which bigotry has endeavored to create against them."[95] Despite the periodically violent anti-Catholicism of the years leading up to the Civil War, Irish Catholics in Genesee County enjoyed a peace and acceptance often absent in an America witnessing the rise of the Know Nothing Party and its continuous assault on the place of Catholics in American life.

Therefore, the Irish immigrants who greeted Father Dillon in LeRoy in 1849 welcomed a resident priest to the town by 1868, Father Daniel DeLacy Moore.[96] Over the next several decades, Catholicism in Genesee County expanded and deepened in a manner illustrative of a church that, as in Ireland, functioned as an institution in which the emotional and political bond between the clergy and the people remained pronounced. At least initially, Catholic populism was indistinguishable from Irish populism, and this remained a dominant trait into the latter part of the nineteenth century and beyond, when that same church received an influx of Catholics from other parts of the world who brought histories, traditions and views of the world markedly different from those of the Irish. Nevertheless, the role of some of these ethnic groups, particularly the Italian and the Polish Catholics—and their relationship with a church hierarchy dominated by the Irish—is one that would take us beyond this chapter. As in late nineteenth-century Genesee County, a major challenge for the church remained the absorption of many different peoples with a multitude of histories and traditions, all struggling to find a home within the broader context of Roman Catholicism.

The descendants of those initial Irish immigrants in the county adjusted to the changing realities of not only the Roman Catholic Church but also

Irish entrepreneurs in Batavia, early 1920s.

An example of mainstream Genesee County society. Pictured is a lower-middle-class family of unknown ethnicity in Genesee County in the early twentieth century.

to the wider county society. They enjoyed a growing social acceptance, as indicated by movement into county positions of leadership. By 1915, Irish Americans occupied such positions as the chief of police, fire chief, and head postmaster in Batavia.[97]

Irish Americans rose rapidly from their initial poverty and marginalization to become not only community leaders but also accepted members of mainstream Genesee County society.

As a group, they achieved the dream of their ancestors in the 1830s and 1840s: assimilation into the county and American society. Their fate is akin to that of another immigrant group in Genesee County's history, the Italians.

THE ITALIANS

Italian immigrants such as Paolo Busti made their presence felt in Genesee County as early as the late eighteenth century. Busti worked as the Holland Land Company's agent general, orchestrating real estate transactions in western New York on behalf of Dutch investors.[98] However, it was not until the late nineteenth and early twentieth centuries that larger numbers of Italian immigrants began to arrive in the county. Prior to this period,

Italian immigration was negligible. But with the increase in Italian immigration, a response to the labor demands of railroads such as the New York Central, along with such mines as United States Gypsum by the early twentieth century, an estimated 250 Italians lived in Batavia alone. Their origins, and the initial reaction of the non-Italian community, were typical of what these more recent immigrants faced elsewhere in the United States by the closing decades of the nineteenth century.[99] How those early reactions eventually changed and how the descendants of those immigrants ultimately became an integral part of Genesee County and the country at large is a story still unfolding today.

The first Italian immigrants to arrive in large numbers were typically peasants from southern Italy. Intent on building a life free from hunger, political tyranny, and rampant economic exploitation, they also tended to idealize America—until they disembarked at Ellis Island and confronted harsher realities than those they anticipated. Such harshness took numerous forms, including organized violence directed against them by such groups as the Ku Klux Klan.

Nonetheless, for reasons that will be discussed, the early images of Italian immigrants that were largely negative subsequently yielded to far more flattering images that, over time, afforded opportunities to descendants that could not have been imagined by the immigrant generation. The Italian American image that developed out of the hard work, patience, and suffering of those first arrivals eventually produced descendants who thought of themselves as Americans—though Americans with Italian ancestry. But that is getting ahead of ourselves. To understand what eventually came to be, one needs to step back in time and explore the lives of these earliest Italian immigrants to Genesee County and the world they left behind in Italy.

THE IMMIGRANTS

The bulk of Italian immigrants departed an impoverished agricultural area, one in which malnutrition, hunger, political corruption, and tyranny, natural disasters and epidemics were the norm. Even by European standards, the peasants of the Mezzogiorno, or southern Italy, were exploited. For example, in 1902, common laborers in Sicily earned the equivalent of $0.25 cents for twelve hours of backbreaking labor. By contrast, in that same year, urban workers in the United States realized between $1.50 and $2.00 per day. An excerpt from a southern Italian folk song in this period captures the anger and resentment of many immigrants:

> *Today, landlord, you will plow*
> *your own field*
> *Because we are leaving*
> *for America.*[100]

For many immigrants, the vision of America was that of a promised land, an earthly paradise holding forth the possibility of dignity and security—aspects of life not attainable in the towns, cities, and fields of Italy.

Conversely, Americans held their own impressions of Italy. In the nineteenth century, there emerged two views of Italy.[101] The earlier perspective—evident prior to the mass migration of rural Italians in the late 1800s—was quite positive. Italy was as much an idea as a nation in this view, for it embodied the finest of Western traditions—political idealism, artistic sensitivity, intellectual creativity, and worldly experience. People such as the critic Henry James flocked to Italy in search of the rich experiences found there. So, too, did writers like James Fennimore Cooper and Nathaniel Hawthorne. In Genesee County, the beauty of Italian culture appeared in such newspapers as the *Spirit of the Times*. For instance, in an 1825 issue, an extended discussion of the collections in the Museum of Naples appeared. The writer of this article spoke of the delicate intricacy of the jewelry from antiquity on display. "I assure you," readers learned, "that our most skillful jewelers could make nothing more elegant, or a better taste."[102]

However, the admiration discernible in earlier depictions of Italy had all but vanished by the early twentieth century, with the arrival of 2,045,877 Italian immigrants by 1910 (although 1,154,322 of these people eventually returned to Italy). Despite the high remigration, the fact remains that this movement of mostly southern Italians was a dramatic shift in the history of Italian migration. In the ten-year period between 1860 and 1870, a mere 12,000 Italians departed for the United States. However, after 1870, the Italian ceased to be an abstraction. Previously, most Americans had never encountered an Italian. If they thought of Italians at all, it was through the eyes of American writers, including those mentioned and many more, such as the feminist and political activist Margaret Fuller, who praised the political ideals of the revolutionary Giuseppe Mazzini, one of the architects of the modern Italian state.[103]

Instead, by the close of the nineteenth century, the typical American met face to face the southern Italian peasant, who tended to be illiterate and unskilled. In addition, southern Italian immigrants arrived at a moment of intense racial stereotyping, where Anglo-Saxons stood at the top of a social hierarchy and Italians came to occupy the lower rungs of this racial pecking order, with the lowest rungs occupied by African Americans. Combined with the poverty of peasants willing to work at low-paying occupations because of clear necessity, yet another factor that worked to the Italian immigrant's disadvantage was the alleged propensity to engage in radical politics based on class conflict. For many in democratic America, this seemed inappropriate. In Genesee County, nowhere was this more evident than in Oakfield in 1905 and 1906 at the United States Gypsum Company.[104]

THE CONFRONTATION
AT THE UNITED STATES GYPSUM COMPANY

A farmer in Oakfield discovered "land plaster," or gypsum, in 1825. Shortly afterward, a mine commenced operations, along with a grinding mill. The mine eventually became the largest narrow-vein mine in the world. As demand for a material used to make plaster, blackboard chalk and wallboard grew, so too did the use of power-driven machines in the Oakfield mine. By 1902, the United States Gypsum Company had been established.[105]

The need for more miners in order to meet the demand for gypsum translated into reliance on Italian immigrants willing to endure the dangers of gypsum mining—an endeavor in which the roof of the gypsum mine could easily collapse despite efforts to support the limestone roof layer. On November 2, 1905, a collapse of this sort is exactly what happened.

Just before noon on that day, a roof collapsed and killed two miners. One of them, Gaetano Valente, was a thirty-year-old immigrant.[106] On the following day at United States Gypsum, approximately two hundred miners who were also Italian immigrants walked off the job and proclaimed their intention never to enter the gypsum mines again.[107] In December, readers of Batavia's *Daily News* were informed that "several of the company's miners" boarding at the residence maintained by the company "were drunk and creating a great disturbance."[108] The following day, the *Daily News* continued its coverage of developments at the boardinghouse, now mentioning thefts that had occurred there.[109]

Main Street, Batavia, shortly before the Gypsum Mine unrest, 1902.

While the alleged thieves were not identified as Italian, subsequent depictions of Italians in Genesee County made explicit what was merely implied in the 1905 *Daily News* articles—that Italian immigrants tended to induce social chaos. For example, in the September 12, 1906 issue of the *Daily News*, the front page featured an article about the arrest of "11 Italians…as ringleaders of the rioting discharged by Justice Ingalsbe at Oakfield today," along with discussing a "row among Italians" regarding three families contesting the same well.[110]

The *Daily News* was replete with such stories, and the perceptions of Italian immigrants thus formed were similar to many images generated throughout the United States in this period. However, the negative images of Italian Americans was undermined somewhat by their participation in World War I. Scholars have estimated that about 12 percent of the U.S. Army comprised both Italian immigrants and the sons of immigrants born in the United States. Two received the Congressional Medal of Honor, while another one hundred received the Distinguished Service Cross. Italian immigrants who fought in the American military were granted United States citizenship while still serving. The negative images of Italian Americans that persisted despite their participation in World War I is also indicative of the wider

This page, top: Unidentified children in Oakfield at the time of the Gypsum Mine unrest, 1905.

This page, bottom: Postcard showing Main Street in Oakfield at the time of the Gypsum Mine unrest.

Opposite, top: Downtown Oakfield in 1908, three years after the Gypsum Mine unrest.

Opposite, bottom: A wagon with children in Oakfield, shortly after the Gypsum Mine strike.

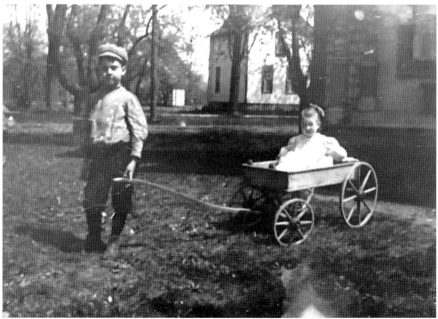

U.S. Gypsum plant by the 1930s.

trepidation regarding workers in general as America entered the twentieth century, as historians such as Steven J. Ross have pointed out in an analysis of silent film depictions of class conflict. In any event, despite the sacrifices of Italian workers and their children who served in the First World War, the earlier depictions of chaos associated with Italian immigrants—strikes, the purported propensity for crime, the supposed dangers of Roman Catholicism, and alcohol consumption—all came together in the momentary appeal of the Ku Klux Klan, which by 1924 had achieved national prominence. Its presence on the national stage was evident in areas outside of the Deep South—such as Genesee County. This will be discussed in some detail in chapter 5, although it needs to be at least touched on here.[111]

THE KU KLUX KLAN ATTACK ON ITALIAN AMERICANS

Throughout 1924, anti-Italian sentiments in the county reached a fever pitch. They found concrete expression in the area's Klan activity. The rise of the Klan in Genesee County in the early 1920s was symptomatic of a larger national trend in the period after World War I, which saw a dramatic increase in the numbers of people joining the Klan. The Klan defended a "true Americanism" that excluded African Americans, Roman Catholics, Jews, Mexicans, Asians, and immigrant groups from southern and Eastern Europe—which of course included Italians.

By the time fifty thousand Klan members marched in front of the White House on August 8, 1925, they had helped elect eleven governors and briefly controlled the state legislatures of Colorado, Oregon, Texas, and Oklahoma.

In Genesee County, the Klan issued a public statement expressing a desire to march in the Labor Day parade in Batavia in 1924. In August, the *Daily News*, in stories leading up to Labor Day, commented on their presence. One reported that "two open-air ceremonies have been staged by the Batavia realm of the Ku Klux Klan during the past week, one at Morganville on Monday evening and the other at South Alabama on Wednesday evening. Fiery crosses were burned and a class of candidates was initiated at each meeting."[112] Three days later, a front-page article reported a Klan rally in Point Pleasant, New Jersey, attended by four hundred Klan members "in full regalia" who "were listening to a patriotic address by Mrs. Leila Bell."[113] On the next day, the *Daily News* featured a front-page article on the "Midnight Procession of Klansmen" that "moved from Batavia to Indian Falls for Ku Klux Initiation Ceremonies."[114] All of this culminated in an August 21

Building used by Polish and Italian Catholics as a church in the early twentieth century.

Some of the St. Anthony's Catholic Church parishioners in Batavia in the 1930s.

Main and Bank Streets in Batavia, as second-generation Italian Americans came of age, 1920.

headline in that same newspaper announcing, "Thousands of Klansmen Are to Hold a Picnic Labor Day in Batavia."[115]

As Labor Day approached, opposition to the Klan's plan appeared. On August 23, a *Daily News* article noted opposition in the county against the use of public parks for Klan events.[116] Subsequent articles through Labor Day emphasized the intensity of the controversy surrounding the Klan's call for a gathering in Batavia. Through the end of August, the *Daily News* acknowledged receipt of letters signed with such phrases as "A Batavia Klanswoman," in which Roman Catholics were denounced. Despite this controversy, on September 2 the Klan gathered at Exposition Park. Public lectures featured talks regarding such topics as "One Country, One Language, One Flag."[117]

The resultant anxiety expressed by such Catholic leaders as Father William C. Kirby was the low point of the Italian experience in Genesee County. Fears for the physical safety of Italian immigrants and their children were understandable, for it was only thirty-three years earlier, in New Orleans that the largest mass lynching in United States history occurred. In this incident, eleven Italian immigrants were murdered.[118] Given the intensity of hostility displayed against Italians and other groups lying outside of the Klan's "100 percent Americanism," such as Irish Catholics—who were also considered "alien" by the Klan due to their "foreignness" and Catholicism—an obvious question arises. How and when did portrayals of Italian immigrants and their descendants change? This brings us to the nature of a rural area such as Genesee County and the tremendous impact of the Second World War.

The Emergence of a New Italian Image

By the late 1940s, two factors combined to alter the perception of Italian immigrants and their offspring in Genesee County. Not surprisingly, these factors appeared nationally. The first was the rural nature of Genesee County. The second was the impact of the Second World War. We will turn first to the rural factor.

Like Italian immigrants making their way west to California in the late nineteenth and early twentieth centuries, Italian migrants to Genesee County integrated themselves into the existing society. This is not to say that they did not encounter discrimination. Instead, southern Italian peasants, who for generations had lived close to the land in sparsely populated areas, found it easier to adapt and commingle with others who also worked the land. Congested urban areas perpetuated and exaggerated ethnic differences in ways that rural areas did not. There was a shared experience among farmers not possible in a city. Rural areas stressed a cooperation that blurred differences between people. The stigma attached to being a foreigner lasted for a shorter time in small farming towns than in a bustling, crowded area such as New York City or New Orleans.

Local media offers examples of just how quickly the image of Italian immigrants and their children had changed by the middle of the twentieth century. This was reflected in such developments as the criminalization of Klan presence in New York State, reported on the front page of the *Daily News* in the summer of 1946.[119]

Stories focusing on rural values—and Italian American farmers embodying those beliefs—abounded in the *Daily News* in the immediate aftermath of the Second World War. Editorials such as "Rural Resourcefulness," appearing in 1946, celebrated the work ethic and innovative spirit of farmers. Readers discovered that "farmers of the Genesee County area still retain much of the resourcefulness of the early settlers when it comes to providing themselves with things they need."[120] Italian American farmers in Elba were the subject of photographic essays. The hard work and innovative techniques of farmers like Patsy Fiorentino and Michael Crope, along with Mrs. Stella Bosco and her son Frank, produced a "bumper onion harvest" in 1946.[121] The rural values featured in such articles combined with the place of the World War II veteran to elevate the children and grandchildren of Italian immigrants to levels of social status unimaginable only a few decades before.

For example, in the late summer of 1946, the *Daily News* introduced readers to Charlie Bishop, a soldier from Batavia who lost his sight as the result of a sniper attack at Yokohoma during the war. He nonetheless undertook the work of his chicken farm after learning how to "feel" his way with his face after spending time at the Army's Old Farm Convalescent Hospital in Connecticut. He learned this along with Joe Baca, a fellow chicken farmer who also lost his sight during the war. Joe, like Charlie, "was taught to 'feel' objects with his face as he approached them, or in the case of moving objects, as they approached him. By feeling the change in air pressure on his face, Joe can, for example, 'feel' the location of a car in the driveway."[122]

Such a positive depiction of an Italian American farmer—and veteran—appeared only two days after the *Daily News* described the ingenuity so prized in rural America on the part of a Batavian who built his own onion topper. Underneath a photograph of Gerald Condello, the caption read, "The dearth of good commercially made farm machinery made Gerald

Condello of Batavia, operator of a large muck land farm, decide to fashion his own onion topping machine."[123] Be it Condello or Baca, such glaringly different depictions of Italian Americans in the local media, in contrast to those of only a generation before, captured the impact of rural life, with its stress on shared values not as evident in crowded, urban conditions. Such depictions also reminded readers of the participation of so many Italian Americans in the war effort. Both of these depictions softened and made socially unacceptable the prejudices so apparent in the earlier part of the century.

This was in keeping with the national pattern. Nearly 1.5 million Italian Americans—about 10 percent of the American military—served in the armed forces during World War II.[124] This made Italian Americans the largest ethnic group to wear American uniforms in that conflict. Two people in particular embodied Italian American participation in the war effort. One was Marine Gunnery Sergeant John Basilone, the only person in American history awarded both of the nation's two highest honors for bravery in combat—the Congressional Medal of Honor and the Navy Cross. Gunnery Sergeant Basilone was killed at Iwo Jima in 1945.[125] The other Italian American embodying the service of so many was Rosie Bonavita, commonly known as "Rosie the Riveter."

Realities such as these meant the end of the older, negative images of Italian Americans and the group's entry into the mainstream of American life by 1945. This shift in public opinion came out in a variety of ways in local publications such as the *Daily News*. By the postwar period, Italian Americans in Genesee County had clearly fulfilled the aspiration to secure a foothold in the mainstream of county life. The *Daily News* provided abundant examples of this. Take just one year—1952. Articles about the inclusion of Italian food in the diet of soldiers fighting in Korea ("Back-Home Spaghetti Treat in Korean War"), along with numerous depictions of Italian American war heroes ("B-29 Crewman Back from Korea Ten Days after Bombing Mill"), appeared. These made their appearance alongside articles on Italian Americans running for the New York State Assembly and receiving academic honors, such as "Batavian Is Graduate of Fredonia College." Another featured a federal official—"New Social Security Officer Is Assigned to Batavia Territory."[126] Such articles are stark testimony to the arrival of the children and grandchildren of Italian immigrants into the middle class.

FROM ITALIANS TO ITALIAN AMERICANS TO AMERICANS

As we move closer to our own day, the stigma once attached to Italian immigrants subsided because of service in World War II and—in the case of Genesee County—the rural realities already discussed. By the 1970s, Italian immigrants had changed into Italian Americans who eventually emerged as Americans of Italian ancestry. While this development is typically visible along generational lines, it is possible to discern it in the life of one person. This is precisely what became visible in a long article in the *Daily News* in 1973. Titled "At 80 Years Old—Mr. Rosica Is Busy Every Day as Shoe Cutter," the article tells the story of Joseph Rosica, whose life embodied the transition from immigrant to American usually discernible in developments between one generation and the next.

Readers learned that Rosica arrived at Ellis Island from the farming village of Pollutri in southern Italy when he was twelve years old. After their arrival in New York City, he and his parents boarded a train for Batavia. Eventually going to work as a shoe cutter for the P.W. Minor and Son Company, Rosica remained there for sixty-three years as of the time of the article. During his first seven years at the factory, he taught himself to read and write, despite never attending school in either Italy or the United States.

He became a draftee with the United States' entry into World War I in 1917. Prior to that, he taught himself how to play the oboe. Since oboe players were few in number, an accomplished local musician and district attorney in Genesee County, William H. Coon, recognized Rosica's talent and encouraged his interest in music. This led to Rosica joining the Batavia Civic Orchestra. When drafted into the army, Coon gave him a letter of recommendation that led to Rosica becoming a permanent member of the Depot Brigade Band at Camp Devens in Massachusetts. He attained the rank of "musician second class."

Upon a return to civilian life and work at the P.W. Minor and Son Company, he joined the American Legion Band and rejoined the Batavia Civic Orchestra. He became a proud homeowner and remained a devoted family man who served as an usher at St. Anthony's Church in Batavia.[127]

The significance of his life is that it is representative of a wider reality in Genesee County and in the nation at large. Like so many others, although typically it developed beyond the immigrant generation, Rosica became indistinguishable from other Americans in terms of income, property ownership and the pursuit of personal interests. In addition, he overcame the discrimination against Italians that had been evident in the county decades earlier. While in some ways maintaining values he brought from rural Italy (Rosica eventually purchased two acres of land to grow crops, thus maintaining the closeness to the land exhibited by Italian agricultural workers), he—like so many other Italian immigrants and their descendants—became an ordinary member of mainstream society. He adopted the ways of Genesee County and America at large, while simultaneously influencing non–Italian America in a multitude of ways.

Be it Genesee County or America at large, the perception of Italians underwent two stages. There was the earlier view of Italians as a people formed in a culture of artistic richness and intellectual vitality. The second image was that of violent and illiterate peasants flooding into states such as New York by the late nineteenth century. A country—and a county—with such a pronounced Protestant theology and culture served to exacerbate suspicions directed toward a largely Roman Catholic immigrant population.

Nevertheless, over time, Italian immigrants and their descendants overcame these prejudices. Military service and rural values facilitated eventual acceptance, tolerance, and respect for hard work, as well as post–World War II disdain for groups such as the Ku Klux Klan. The movement in one generation of an immigrant such as Rosica into the mainstream of community life symbolizes what so many Italian Americans experienced both within and beyond Genesee County by the late twentieth century. The journey that started two centuries earlier culminated in a virtual celebration of what it means to be an American of Italian ancestry in Genesee County. Nowhere is this more apparent than in an award given in the county every year, appropriately called "Italian-American of the Year." The involvement of the individuals given this honor in the county—in activities ranging from Genesee Community College trustee to cancer support groups to YMCA volunteers—is one that immigrants employed by the United States Gypsum Company in the opening decade of the twentieth century could hardly have imagined.

But maybe that is unfair—quite possibly, in their quest for a better life, they could see a future America always in the process of becoming. Maybe that is the biggest lesson of the Irish and Italian journeys in Genesee County—that their history, like the history of our individual lives, is never over. Instead, it is only the continuous process of a person developing in unexpected ways.

CHAPTER 4

HOOVER, ROOSEVELT, AND THE NEW DEAL IN GENESEE COUNTY

Sometimes, my friends, particularly in years such as these,
the hand of discouragement falls upon us. It seems that things are in a rut,
that the world has grown tired and very much out of joint.
This is the mood of depression, of dire and weary depression.
—Franklin D. Roosevelt, "Commonwealth Club Speech," September 23, 1932

The great engineer, self-made man, and leader of the effort to feed starving people in a Europe torn apart by the First World War was inaugurated as the thirty-first president of the United States on March 4, 1929. Herbert Clark Hoover was, not surprisingly, the focus of a front-page story in Batavia's *Daily News* on that date. The optimism felt by many throughout America—and in Genesee County—was embodied in the election to the presidency of a man whose life captured the essence of the American dream. Set in a moment in time featuring what appeared to be surging economic prosperity, Hoover's words on Inauguration Day seemed perfectly reasonable and accurate. As the *Daily News* reminded its readers on that fateful day, Hoover looked forward to the next four years with confidence: "In the large view, we have reached a higher degree of comfort and security than ever existed before in the history of the world. Through liberation from widespread poverty we have reached a higher degree of individual freedom than ever before." The newly inaugurated president continued, "Ours is a land rich in resources, stimulating in its glorious beauty…filled with millions of happy homes blessed with comfort and opportunity."[128]

Yet the apparent serenity about the future expressed by Hoover and the *Daily News* coverage of the inauguration remained undermined by other stories during that same month. These accounts contained a more ominous note and serve to capture the seething economic cauldron bubbling just beneath an apparently tranquil surface. On March 21, a short article reported, "Strikers Denounce Wages of $8.90 a Week." It was accompanied by a dramatic photograph of striking workers on a picket line, carrying signs proclaiming "$8.90 a Week Is Slavery," "Fair Wages or No Wages," "United We Stand/Divided We Fall" and "$15.00 or Bust." The caption below the photo read, "Strikers from the Flanzstoff rayon plant in Elizabethton, Tenn., parading through the streets protesting low wages are pictured above…Most of the marchers were girls and women."[129]

Such displays by poorly paid factory workers stood in stark contrast to the hopeful optimism exhibited by Hoover and the overall tone of the press coverage in the *Daily News*. So, too, did other stories appearing that same month in the *Daily News*, although their ominous nature was not as immediately recognizable at a moment when the economy appeared to be "roaring." Five days later, on March 26, the *Daily News* featured a front-page article that reported, "The stock market broke wide open again today when the call money rate was jacked up to 20 per cent, the highest level in nine years.…The money stringency was the tightest since July 1, 1920 and was attributed to a combination of circumstances. While loans called by banks only amounted to $25,000,000 there was no new money coming into the market. Out-of-town withdrawals were heavy, especially by Chicago interests to support the market there."[130]

The very mention of "call money" indicates just how volatile the economic picture was beneath the deceptive calm. An overheated economy, one in which banks lent money repayable on demand in the absence of a fixed repayment schedule, indicates that an individual's prosperity was misleading. Juxtaposed next to the images of a boundlessly optimistic incoming presidential administration were wages either stagnant or in decline. This translated into a recipe for a collapse not seen in American life since the deep economic depression of the early 1890s. Indeed, the economic collapse of October 1929 produced an economic downturn that was unprecedented.

While the focus here is the *political* response to the Great Depression in Genesee County, the stage must nonetheless be set. The stakes in the 1932 presidential election were extraordinarily high. The hard times in the county in 1932 were a microcosm of the nation's agony in that pivotal year.

The causes of the Great Depression easily take us beyond the scope of this chapter. Suffice it to say that the stock market crash of October 1929—a month in which stock values on the New York Stock Exchange fell an average of 37 percent—was the consequence of reckless speculation and an overextension of credit throughout the 1920s. Speculation was seemingly everywhere—in Florida real estate and in stock purchases—all at a time in which wages for typical Americans revealed a downward trend. Americans were nonetheless all too willing to overextend themselves through the purchase of stocks "on margin" in an effort to get rich quick. In other words, they charged their stock purchases in the hope that the value of the stock would rise and they could sell for a profit. Simultaneously, there was a flagrant misdistribution of wealth—by 1929, economic historians conclude that approximately one-third of all personal income in the United States had been accumulated by a mere 5 percent of the population.

This growing concentration of wealth in fewer hands combined with stagnant wages and unbridled speculation to artificially inflate stock prices. The collapse became inevitable. With that breakdown, confidence in the market waned. People rushed to banks to withdraw monies in uninsured accounts. Banks that had loaned money for speculative purposes eventually, by the end of 1929, revealed the deceptive prosperity. The economy began its steep and rapid descent, a contraction leaving in its wake vast amounts of human suffering.

By the presidential election of 1932, the country found itself in the midst of an acute crisis—13 million Americans were unemployed in a nation of a little more than 91 million. By 1933, the national unemployment rate stood at 25 percent. Such figures are suggestive of the amount and type of suffering common in the United States in 1932. In states such as Kentucky and West Virginia, evicted coal miners and their families found themselves living in tents in the midst of winter. Many of their children lacked shoes. In Los Angeles, people whose electricity and gas had been disconnected found themselves cooking over wood fires in back lots. A Philadelphia storekeeper revealed to a reporter that he was extending credit to a family of eleven. He said that this family had children without shoes or pants. Their house did not even have chairs. Somewhere between 1 million and 2 million people roamed the country in search of work. In Chicago, 50 hungry men fought over a barrel of garbage set outside a restaurant's back door. The commissioner of charity in Salt Lake City reported that "scores" of people were slowly starving—while hundreds of children remained out of school because of a lack of clothing.

The national anguish was evident in Genesee County. By the winter of 1930, the *Daily News* reported that a grand jury had indicted an ex-banker from Bergen named Charles E. Housel, who was "charged with feloniously receiving deposits in an insolvent bank."[131] Two months later, the *Daily News* reported on the tragic consequences of financial hardship in yet another of numerous articles along these lines, in an article headlined "Hume MacPherson, Bergen Native, Killed Wife with Ax, Then Himself, Money Troubles Probable Cause." The article noted the middle-class character of the couple, who were "both college graduates":

> *Discouraged over financial issues, Hume MacPherson, 46, of Detroit, Michigan, a former Bergen resident, killed his 45-year-old wife with an axe and then took his own life by carbon-monoxide poisoning in the garage in the rear of their Piedmont Avenue home in Detroit. Word of the murder and suicide, which took place Thursday, was received in this village today. Mr. MacPherson was a son of the late D.J. MacPherson, who was a correspondent for the* Daily News *for forty years.*[132]

Three months later, the *Daily News* featured advertisements for the New York State Bankers Association. It had established a Bandit Reward Fund, which offered a reward for aid in the capture of bank robbers "dead or alive."[133] By December 1930, as economic conditions worsened, readers were offered a front-page article about a Wyoming, New York resident who was earning his living by peddling candy from a goat cart: "Batavians were greeted with a novel plan of facing the unemployment situation several days ago. His only means of support for his family being his small cart, drawn by a sturdy 'Billy' goat, and a supply of candy made with goat's milk."[134]

In 1931, economic conditions continued to deteriorate with no end in sight. In late 1931, the *Daily News* reported, "400 Under-Nourished Children Largely in Families Whose Parents Are Too Proud to Ask for Aid Will Receive Help from the Red Cross."[135] Two weeks later, a man from Pavilion "who admitted stealing a sheep gave hunger as the reason for the act." The court took into account his terrible economic conditions. He therefore received a suspended sentence.[136]

The deepening of the Great Depression through the early months of 1932 only brought a flood of unrelenting bad economic news. In late January, the *Daily News* reported that "Shirt Workers Went on Strike" at the factory of Joseph Horowitz and Sons in Batavia because of a 15 percent wage cut. This reduced an already paltry compensation of $1.60 per day even lower.[137]

New York State troopers in Batavia to quell a strike in 1933.

Depressed wages, hunger, high unemployment, reports of bankruptcies, and family disarray linked to economic pressure all characterized *Daily News* articles throughout 1932. By that summer and fall, a demoralized population wondered what, if any, political changes might alter the dire economic situation. On July 8, the *Daily News* published a sermon by Reverend Elmer Harris of Bethany's Baptist Church titled "Why Do We Have Poverty?"[138] That same newspaper—a mere four days before the presidential election—reminded readers of just how volatile the political terrain had become, when it set forth the five presidential candidates appearing on the ballot in Genesee County:

- Republican—Herbert Hoover
- Democrat—Franklin D. Roosevelt
- Socialist—Norman Thomas
- Social Labor—Verne L. Reynolds
- Communist—William Z. Foster[139]

Therefore, it is not surprising that the demoralization seen in the public was suddenly set aside on Election Day, November 8. A front-page article in the *Daily News*, headlined "Voting Rush in This City Near Record…More than 5,000 Votes Cast in Batavia by 1:30 This Afternoon," offered a dramatic depiction of just how motivated voters were as a consequence of the massive economic stakes and in spite of the previous summer's demoralization.[140] Even more stunning were the front-page *Daily News* stories of November 9. At a moment in which Franklin Roosevelt won every state except for Pennsylvania, Connecticut, Vermont, New Hampshire, and Maine, and as *Daily News* headlines proclaimed a "Tremendous Victory for the Democrats," Genesee County favored Hoover by more than five thousand votes. In addition, county voters elected every Republican candidate running for office in the county by what the *Daily News* called "wide margins."[141] What is the explanation here? In part, the answer to this question lies in what Hoover embodied for many in the county despite the bleak economic conditions.

PRESIDENT HOOVER
AND THE IMAGE OF AN EARLIER TIME

One of the more extraordinary realities in human history is the powerful effect of political imagery. Political images are often as decisive in the way people vote as the economic realities they face. Therefore, despite dire economic conditions, Hoover and the Republican Party enjoyed astounding political success in Genesee County in November 1932, while the remainder of the country largely rejected them in the wake of the economic collapse. The key to comprehending Hoover's continued popularity in the county is that his life and beliefs embodied local values. Admiration for him and his party's core beliefs remained, despite the economic hurricane of the Great Depression.

In the wake of Hoover's nomination as the Republican Party candidate in 1928, there was an enthusiastic outpouring of praise for this self-made man. Indeed, on the day the party's convention in Kansas City, Missouri, ended, the *Daily News* featured a timeline of Hoover's life complete with photographs. Readers of the June 15, 1928, issue learned:

> *At 6, an Iowa Blacksmith's son.*
> *At 12, an orphan, taken to Oregon by an Uncle.*
> *At 21, Graduated from College—Worked His Way.*
> *In 1900, helped other Americans defend Tientsin during the Boxer Rebellion (in China)…*
> *By 1910, a World-Famous Mining Engineer. In War (World War One), Directed World-Wide Relief Work.*[142]

On the day the convention ended, the *Daily News* featured photographs of Hoover's parents and their modest, rural home. "From this humble farm home at West Branch, Iowa," the *Daily News* told readers, "Herbert Hoover fought his way through life's obstacles to one of the most important positions in the national life of the country."[143] The adulation continued unabated. On June 20, 1928, the paper featured photographs of rural West Branch, "Herbert Hoover's Birthplace,"[144] that drove home the obvious point: that Hoover's life of modest beginnings, hard work, and persistence was the very essence of what is best in America—and in Genesee County.

Even the disruption caused by the Great Depression could not alter what many in the county believed about themselves, their community, and the nation. Hoover and the Republican Party stood for free enterprise, opportunity, personal achievement, material well-being, and a peace achieved through the energetic pursuit of business success devoid of governments tending to impede progress and even generate war. Few forgot Hoover's work as a food administrator during and after World War I. Rather than participating in the killing of others, he had directed efforts to feed and house those finding themselves homeless in war-ravaged Europe. Here was a successful and compassionate humanitarian motivated to create a general social good inseparable from one's self-interest. Hoover's altruism, based on *voluntary* cooperation between people (as opposed to government-compelled programs), struck a particularly receptive audience in Genesee County. This was part of his image. He could be trusted with the presidency and would use it to advance both domestic progress and international peace. Even the severity of the Great Depression did not weaken his hold on many in Genesee County. This included religious leaders. In 1932, the official journal of the *Genesee Annual Conference of the Methodist Episcopal Church* expressed its fervent support for President Hoover, remarking on his personal character, "Be it resolved that this conference is pleased to place itself on record in appreciation of the untiring personal devotion of the President of these United States to the high ideals of Patriotism and Humanity. It recognizes his personal sincerity, his practical sagacity, his political consistency, his moral integrity, and his truly Christian spirit, in public presentation and controversy."[145]

The support of the Methodist Episcopal Church in Genesee County remained inseparable from the wide support Hoover enjoyed throughout the county despite the severity of the economic downturn. Four days before Election Day, the *Daily News* eschewed any semblance of subtlety in an editorial titled "Go to the Polls!" It was not Hoover's lack of personal capacity that caused the Depression, for Hoover possessed an aptitude for the presidency that as a self-made man he had spent a lifetime developing. Unfortunately, the editorial writer reasoned, the America he grew up in had essentially collapsed with an unexpected suddenness during his first year in office. Nonetheless, there was no reason to reject an entire way of life. That way of life included a belief in limited government, self-reliance, and voluntary cooperation between people, in contrast to government-mandated programs. A man whose personal success resulted from that way of life deserved to be president. Hence, the editorial writer said, "There are about three times as many Republicans in Genesee County as there are Democrats, and if the Republicans will go to the polls next Tuesday and vote for the nominees of their party, all of whom merit their hearty support, Old Genesee will roll up a magnificent majority for Hoover and [Vice President Charles] Curtis and aid materially in the triumphant re-election of these stalwart standard-bearers." The editorial continued, "It is just a question of getting out to vote—and voting right. This is not the time to experiment in government. President Hoover knows his job. It would be a tremendous mistake to take him from it."[146]

Expressing political feelings deeply held throughout Genesee County, and which proved decisive on Election Day, the *Daily News* articulated what many felt. The Great Depression, for all of its horror, could prove to be the most damaging in the end if it gave birth to the abandonment of a social philosophy about the proper role of government that had long served the people well. However, national opinion was clearly moving in a different direction within the context of 25 percent unemployment. Ironically, it was the New York governor Franklin Delano Roosevelt who successfully argued that the seriousness of the economic crisis demanded the very thing explicitly rejected in the aforementioned editorial: governmental experimentation. Economic crisis or not, Genesee County Republicans understood that to mean a radical alteration in the relationship between the people and their government. While Republicans endorsing Hoover were reluctant to accept such a proposal, others in the county, even among some Republicans, were not. For them, as for members of other political parties in the county, Hoover belonged to an earlier America no longer in existence. Change was needed, such people argued, and it was needed immediately.

ROOSEVELT, THE NEW DEAL,
AND THE WILLINGNESS TO EXPERIMENT

As many historians and economists have long acknowledged, Roosevelt, though privately a moderate conservative, nonetheless viewed the economic crisis as one demanding immediate, innovative approaches. As he clearly put it, "The country needs and, unless I mistake its temper, the country demands bold, persistent experimentation. It is common sense to take a method and try it. If it fails, admit it frankly and try another. But above all, try something."[147] Along with Roosevelt's insistence on immediate action, he also viewed the American economic system—capitalism—as one that had matured. Hoover's continuous advocacy of individual initiative and unlimited opportunity belonged to an earlier age, at least as Roosevelt saw it. For Roosevelt, the maturing of the American economic system meant large concentrations of wealth in a few hands, and those "economic royalists" could not be trusted to pursue policies benefiting the country as a whole. As he put it in yet another speech, "The unfeeling statistics of the past three decades show that the independent businessman is running a losing race...Recently a careful study was made of the concentration of business in the United States. It showed that our economic life was dominated by some six hundred odd corporations who controlled two-thirds of American industry." Roosevelt pointed out that such a trend threatened American democracy: "If the process goes on at the same rate, at the end of another century we shall have all American industry controlled by a dozen corporations, and run by perhaps a hundred men." He said, "All this calls for a re-appraisal of values...The day of enlightened administration has come."[148]

Therefore, the new president sought both to experiment *and* to design a system that rationally managed the American economy. On the one hand, the New Deal was a radical response emphasizing experimentation. Nonetheless, the New Deal also recognized that a concentration of economic power was here to stay. For Roosevelt, the challenge was to find a way to manage wealth that already existed and distribute it as evenly as possible throughout American society, while retaining the essential features of the capitalist marketplace. This was a tall order in Republican Genesee County. The burning political question was how it would be received.

This brings us to the spring of 1933 and the arrival of the New Deal in Genesee County. In March of that year, the new president moved quickly to halt the deepening of the economic downturn. One of the first actions of the new administration was to stop the withdrawal of funds from banks. In this pre-FDIC (Federal Deposit Insurance Corporation) era, many Americans had lost their life savings because of bank failures. On March 9, Roosevelt asked Congress to declare a four-day bank holiday in order to reduce the panic of depositors by precluding their ability to withdraw funds. Congress only took seven hours to pass the Emergency Banking Relief Act. Newspaper reports about the county's reaction to the bank holiday were uniformly positive. By March 15, the *Daily News*, in an article titled "Every Bank in County Opened for Business," spoke of the optimism of local business leaders and a sense that "every greeting today carried intimation that a better day had dawned."[149]

Along with efforts to stabilize the banking system, that same month featured a new president striving to offer short-term relief to the unemployed. Given the number of unemployed in Genesee County, work relief programs were welcome. "State Highway Work Relief Plan Welcome News to Genesee People," read the *Daily News* headline on March 18.[150] Work relief combined with food relief. Two days later, that same newspaper told readers that "the last carload of flour allotted to Genesee County for relief in Genesee County this winter is being unloaded in this city [Batavia] today."[151]

Another early New Deal effort to revitalize the economy and restore hope and confidence to badly shaken Americans was the effort to promote cooperative arrangements between management and employees. Many in the county saw this, too, in a favorable light. An illustration of this is a May 6, 1933 *Daily News* article. "Three Hundred Family Men," the newspaper reported, "Will Work for State Next Week." Here, we see a cooperative venture that included business and governmental collaboration: "On the days assigned to them to start work, the men are to report to receiving points for transportation to the job. The list of 300 is divided as follows: Attica State Prison farm 158; Western New York Egg Laying Plant at Stafford 25; Batavia-Bergen road 117."[152]

This effort to foster cooperation extended to a wide variety of county residents from different occupations, including county barbers. In an advertisement in the summer of 1933 in support of the National Recovery Administration (NRA)—a New Deal effort to stabilize the economy via uniform prices and wages—"The Barbers of Batavia" told the community, "Master and Journeymen Barbers have accepted the movement of NRA and according to the code which has been accepted by 90 percent of all barbers. We wish to appeal to the people of Batavia to support us in this movement, as we have pledged our support to every movement of the act of the NRA in so doing to raise the standard of living which means in short all for one, one for all."[153]

When combined with the Roosevelt initiatives to halt the further drop in farm prices through the Agricultural Adjustment Administration (AAA)—a reaction to a decline captured in a *Daily News* article in August 1933 reporting that "farms lost money in '32"—the growing popularity of the New Deal even in Republican Genesee County is clear.[154] Nonetheless, not all in Genesee County supported the New Deal. For example, on October 29, 1936, with the presidential election set for November 3, an advertisement in the *Daily News* read, "Big Republican Parade Monday Night, Nov. 2d. WANTED. 500 Cars Filled with Republicans and Friends to Make This the Biggest Demonstration of Freedom and Democracy Ever Held in Genesee County. $50.00 in Prizes Given for the Best Three Floats Opposing the Policies of the New Deal—Enter Yours."[155]

By October 31, the *Daily News* had officially endorsed the Republican challenger for the presidency, Kansas governor Alf Landon: "The Republican ticket to be voted upon Tuesday is one which deserves the support of everyone interested in the preservation of America for Americans by Americans." The Republican ticket features "candidates who believe this country can be successfully run by following the precepts of law and order rather than the dreams of theory and recklessness."[156] The intensity displayed by the eve of Election Day played itself out in that same October 31 issue. An enormous advertisement promoting the New Deal rested alongside a Republican rejection of the Roosevelt policies. "Keep Going with ROOSEVELT" featured "Facts to Remember!" These included a reduction of unemployment by 27 percent, an increase in steel production by 338 percent, a rise in net farm income by 141 percent and an increase in bank deposits by 38 percent.[157]

By the time votes were counted, Roosevelt had received a national mandate on the New Deal. He won every state except for Vermont and Maine. Nonetheless, in Genesee County, he lost.[158] Landon received 13,131 votes in the county, while 6,076 cast their ballots for Roosevelt. There is an irony here that cannot be ignored. In this steadfastly Republican county, New Deal contributions remain popular to this day. A stark example of this is the Works Progress Administration monies that poured into the county during the 1930s. This funding made possible the widening of Main Street in Batavia, a road improvement still visible today. That funding also built the popular MacArthur Park in Batavia and remodeled the county courthouse. These are only some of the examples of New Deal money readily accepted and used in Genesee County by the late 1930s.[159] Despite the Republican victory in Genesee County, the *Daily News* editorialized the day after the election that given the national landslide in favor of Roosevelt, one must acknowledge that "the people of America…believe in the type of leadership which is willing to try almost anything once."[160] With the storm clouds of war already appearing in Europe and Asia, that willingness to experiment placed the New Deal in a different light by the end of the 1930s. Because of this altered perception, there emerged a different sense of the New Deal's meaning, even among staunch Republican opponents of Roosevelt's domestic policies.

The New Deal as a Moderate Response in a Decade of Political Extremes

The New Deal emerged in a decade characterized by political extremes. The Great Depression in the United States was part of a global economic crisis in the 1930s. In other nations, political responses to the Depression were marked by political policies having, as their starting point, a rejection of a democratic system seemingly to blame for the human misery produced by the virtual collapse of capitalism. Free markets, representative legislatures, civil rights and individual political freedoms came under assault in one country after another. Germany and Italy come to mind, but many other nations joined in this assault to one degree or another. On the opposite side of the political spectrum, there stood the Soviet Union. In its case, the rejection of representative legislatures and free markets—not to mention individual political freedoms—vanished when the Bolsheviks seized power in 1917.

In the United States, despite the New Deal, such political extremes also emerged. In Detroit, a group calling itself the Black Legion saw thirteen of its members receive life sentences for the murder of their opponents. This included the killing of Charles A. Poole, a New Deal official kidnapped from his home and murdered. Their other enemies included Roman Catholics, African Americans, and Jews. At a fascist camp in Narrowsburg, New York, Christian Fronters undertook rifle practice using a likeness of Roosevelt's head as a target. In February 1939, twenty thousand American Nazis held a rally in New York City's Madison Square Garden, denouncing the New Deal as a "Jew Deal."[161] Great economic stress intensified political fanaticism, as some sought simple answers in response to complex economic problems.

Violent political militancy was therefore as much a national problem in the United States as it was abroad. However, in Genesee County, the challenges expressed toward the New Deal did not produce the kind of militant violence seen in Detroit or even in other areas of New York, such as Narrowsburg in southern New York's Sullivan County. In fact, as the decade developed, the New Deal, if anything, was understood as part of an American consensus about the value of democracy. Even Republican opponents of Roosevelt's policies applauded the administration for capturing the essence of a humanitarian and compassionate centrism while avoiding the radicalism of fascism on the far right and authoritarian communism on the far left. For Genesee County residents, Republicans and Democrats disagreed about how to *organize* freedom, but individual liberty remained the ultimate goal. Such an objective was especially dramatic in a decade featuring a growth of state power routinely crushing the individual in places such as Germany, Spain, Italy, Japan, and the Soviet Union, to name but a few nations.

Therefore, many editorials in the *Daily News*—despite its consistent support of Republican candidates generally opposed to the New Deal— articulated a celebration of why American democracy was superior to many foreign political systems. Editorials throughout the 1930s celebrated the freedoms enjoyed by Americans in general and Genesee County residents in particular. In the fall of 1938, one such editorial, titled "Two Systems of Rule," alluded to the partition of Czechoslovakia and commented, "Perhaps one of the most beneficial results of the events which have just taken place in Europe is the demonstration…of the difference between how the ruler of a democracy and a dictator approaches his people after an important event." The editorial goes on: "The dictators of Italy and Germany went home and told their subjects what they did and, except for the expected ritualistic acclaims, that was all there was to it.…On the other hand, the French premier went home to a hectic situation with his parliament. He had to explain what happened.…The Premier of Great Britain had even more difficulties. He was and still is being subjected to a severe heckling." The conclusion in this editorial was that a democracy is disorderly and contentious, but it is, nonetheless, a just vehicle for expressing the many opinions of its people. New Deal or not, the editorial writer reminded the readership, "There can be no hesitation by Americans in choosing between the two systems and in deciding to do all that each and all of us can to preserve the democratic form for this country."[162]

On the following day, the *Daily News* stated in yet another editorial, "The welfare of the nation demands that differences be settled and that the energies of all American institutions and their leaders be turned toward the one vital problem of promoting welfare for all Americans regardless of the lesser interests of any particular organization or personalities."[163] Editorials by a clearly Republican-leaning newspaper not consistently sympathetic to the Roosevelt administration nevertheless accepted the contentiousness produced by New Deal policies. This was an acceptable price to pay for the maintenance of a democratic system clearly rejecting the political fanaticism visible in the 1930s. For example, an October 1938 editorial titled "Let's Be Americans" offered an understanding of a decade characterized by extreme political polarization: "We are beset on all sides with troubling events and bombardments against American traditions. We are confronted with a world-wide struggle between the forces of democracy and those of totalitarianism."[164] It is therefore not surprising that this periodical featured stories regarding the threat to democracy by both the far right and the far left at a time of international economic distress. On October 11, 1938, a front-page article appeared regarding an American Nazi rally producing a riot in New Milford, New Jersey.[165] Three days later, a story titled "Kiwanis Speaker Hits Communism" described a talk warning of the dangers of communism, especially at a moment in which people could be tempted to try it because of the failures of capitalism. "Communism," D.J. Leary of the Buffalo Kiwanis said, "would be purchased at the price of freedom."[166] While the New Deal was not perfect, it pursued a safe, middle-of-the-road course in a decade featuring a negation of individual freedom. There was a degree of urgency in this defense of American democracy. After all, among the political parties featured on Genesee County ballots in the off-year elections of November 1938 was the Communist Party.

The essential compassion and decency inherent in American democratic institutions capable of producing such reforms as the New Deal stood in stark contrast to the evil produced by the negation of individual freedoms practiced in authoritarian regimes. As the trampling of individual rights intensified in Nazi Germany, the *Daily News* accelerated its editorials and stories about what this meant in human terms and how utterly different such policies were when compared to American beliefs. For instance, there was *Kristallnacht*, or the "Night of Broken Glass," in Germany (November 9 and 10, 1938), when hundreds of German and Austrian Jews were murdered, thirty thousand Jewish men were placed in concentration camps, about one thousand synagogues were burned and more than seven thousand Jewish businesses and an untold number of schools, hospitals, and homes were destroyed by mob violence. The *Daily News* featured editorials and descriptions about how this contrasted with American civilization. On November 14, an editorial castigating the "unbelievable ferocity and barbarity" of *Kristallnacht*

The continued presence of the Roosevelts in Genesee County: James Roosevelt, son of FDR, with Batavia's Mayor Gabriel in the 1950s.

concluded that it was the unchecked totalitarianism of Adolf Hitler's regime that produced "a policy that shames the nation in the eyes of the world."[167] Two days before Christmas in 1938, another editorial in the *Daily News* stressed that communism and fascism both fed on "the prevalence of poverty" that "gives the agitator his first chance." In the United States, the remedy for totalitarianism was a reform of capitalism fashioned to facilitate as much opportunity as possible. More individual freedom coupled with just the right amount of government involvement held the potential for the emergence of a more just and stable society. The newspaper editorialized that "those now in a position to do so bend their efforts toward preserving our liberties, keeping us informed and giving all who are able the chance to earn a decent living."[168]

This raises the obvious question: was the New Deal, as a moderate reform effort in a very tough 1930s, successful? Asking that question with regard to Genesee County means thinking about an implied question: was the New Deal successful nationally? Just as importantly, did residents see it as a success in Genesee County?

DID THE PEOPLE OF GENESEE COUNTY SEE THE NEW DEAL AS SUCCESSFUL?

On the eve of the 1940 presidential election, Republican presidential candidate Wendell L. Willkie visited Batavia. He received an enthusiastic reception on October 16. An estimated crowd of ten thousand welcomed this stalwart opponent of the New Deal with chants of "We want Willkie."[169] The essential thrust of Willkie's opposition to the New Deal was one that resonated with many in the county. His campaign articulated what many in Genesee County feared, Great Depression or not. The New Deal, for its county detractors, was the negation of a cherished American notion to which Hoover had devoted an entire book in 1922: *American Individualism*. "Willkie," the *Daily News* told its readers on October 19, "Fears U.S. Socialism in F.D.R. Trend."[170] For many, a rejection of individualism was a leap to political extremism. While the middle course of the New Deal may have been tolerable given the alternatives of fascism or communism as a reaction to the crash of 1929, it was hardly a permanent solution—and in and of itself held the potential for ushering in the very totalitarianism characterizing the 1930s.

What did *individualism* mean? Be it Hoover, Willkie, or the typical Republican in Genesee County in 1940, the term referred to a person's freedom of choice. The belief in *individualism* was rooted in the county's Republican culture, and it transcended ethnic differences. It was a view of social organization not peculiar to any one group in the county identifying

The "Willkie Special" at the train station in Batavia in 1940, during the presidential run against FDR. Alongside Willkie is his wife, Edith.

The crowds mobbed his train in Batavia in 1940.

Another photograph of the crowd around Willkie's train in Batavia in 1940.

Close-up photograph of Willkie in Batavia during the 1940 election.

Right: Another portrait of Willkie in Batavia.

Below: Another public figure on the campaign trail in Genesee County—boxing champion Jack Dempsey campaigns for FDR in Batavia in the 1930s.

as Republican, as evidenced by its appearance not only among men but also among Republican women's groups even during the depths of the Depression.[171] It conceived of a self-reliant person. It meant a person working hard for two reasons—the fear of poverty and the promise of opportunity. An individualist rejected the proposition that he or she was owed a living. Along these lines, the support of those in need was the result of a voluntary choice, not governmental coercion. The individualist believed that one's life looked as it looked because of one's own efforts. Therefore, a person must accept the consequences of his or her behavior.

While the New Deal's extensive use of governmental intervention may have been necessary by 1932 in order to avoid the possibility of extreme political reactions, many in the county had always rejected the idea that governmental intervention should be a permanent feature of American life. To make a variety of New Deal programs permanent equaled the normalization of a radically new relationship between individuals and government. In the process, one risked destroying the basic reasons for hard work: fear and opportunity. The social consequences would then be obvious: American society could stagnate because the incentive to work and innovate disappeared.

Therefore, the New Deal would be seen as successful in Genesee County if—and only if—it remained a temporary expedient for pulling the county out of the Great Depression. Herein lay the significance of Roosevelt's policy. The New Deal, rather than being viewed as a radical and permanent departure from the earlier understanding of limited governmental involvement in American lives, should instead be comprehended as a brief interruption in the continuous stress placed on individualism and limited government. The Great Depression was a crisis producing a political abnormality. However, this did not mean that many in the county accepted it as a permanent political realignment. The New Deal was never normal.

Because it was not an ordinary part of county political culture, the underlying value of individualism never disappeared, even with the onslaught of the great economic downturn of the 1930s. This produced the obvious. Liberals, those in the tradition of the New Deal, never fully understood that what they yearned for—a return to what they saw as the "normalcy" of the New Deal after World War II—was a yearning doomed to failure. The foundation of that failure was the continued existence of a belief in individualism and its policy expression of limited government. The idea of limited government had of course changed because of the New Deal—few questioned the desirability of monthly Social Security checks or

Post–New Deal economic recovery. Downtown Batavia, 1950.

federally insured bank accounts. But the essentially conservative nature of Genesee County politics remained unchanged. There is a line of continuity between Herbert Hoover and Ronald Reagan and beyond, a continuum taking us beyond the scope of this chapter.

Was the New Deal successful? Yes, in that it provided a moderate and humane political response to an economic catastrophe. Yes, in that it preserved a free enterprise system necessarily modified to remove its harshest and most unworkable features. And yes, in that it preserved a hallmark of American liberty—individualism. America, and Genesee County, retained its essential Americanism in what proved to be a markedly healthier form. In the wake of the New Deal, American democracy expanded, but it was always an expansion contained within the tradition of the value of individualism. That was especially so in Genesee County. What remains to be seen, as we move deeper into the twenty-first century, is whether the county will retain the belief in limited government that I have stressed throughout this chapter, or whether it will move in a very different direction, as some parts of the country—and New York State—already have.

CHAPTER 5

IN WESTERN NEW YORK?

THE KU KLUX KLAN IN GENESEE COUNTY IN THE 1920S

Apparently, all roads led to Batavia yesterday. Highways in every direction were lined with cars bearing the Klansmen and their invited guests to the city.
—Daily News, *Tuesday, September 2, 1924*

The reader will recall a brief discussion of the Ku Klux Klan in Genesee County in the early 1920s in chapter 3. That discussion was confined to the impact of the Klan on Italian Americans, one of the groups loathed by the Klan in that period. However, the Klan's significance in the early 1920s reached far beyond that one immigrant group. Like the nation at large in the 1920s, the Klan's platform in Genesee County was an expression of the anxiety many felt about a wide range of topics, as we shall see. Its commitment to white supremacy reached beyond the South after World War I, and it did not confine itself to African Americans, who, in any event, formed no more than 3 percent of the entire county population through 1960.[172] Because the African American population remained tiny in the county, other reasons explain the Klan's growth in Genesee County in the early 1920s, as they did for the nation as a whole in this period. It is to those reasons, and their impact and significance locally, that we now turn.

On Labor Day in 1924, at Exposition Park in Batavia, the Klan held a community picnic. Local media reported, "Exposition Park and the streets in the vicinity of it yesterday…had the appearance of a busy day at the Genesee County Fair, for the park was the picnic place of the KU KLUX KLAN of western New York."[173] About fifteen thousand people attended the event. A street parade traveled through downtown Batavia. The festival at Exposition Park embodied much about the Klan's attraction for many in Genesee County during the 1920s. It even suggests something about subsequent life in the county after that decade.

The label of Ku Klux Klan conjures up images drawn from the late nineteenth-century South. That imagery includes African Americans, newly freed from slavery, subject to lynching or other forms of domestic terrorism. However, by the 1920s, that initial Klan activity had largely achieved the goal of Black political and economic subjugation in what remained of the Old South. That same political and economic subjugation also existed in the North. So why do we see Klan resurgence in the 1920s in both the South and in the country at large, including Genesee County, where the vast majority of people were white?

While the Klan in Genesee County continued to stress the exclusion of African Americans, the fact that there were so few people of color in the county demands an exploration of other reasons accounting for the Klan's attraction. A meeting that took place in Batavia's Majestic Hall, during a gathering of the local chapter of the international fraternal organization known as the Odd Fellows, offers a glimpse as to why as many as 3,500 residents of the county joined the Klan in the 1920s and easily twice that number supported its goals. At that assembly, a minister visiting from Macon, Georgia, Reverend Samuel Fowler, spoke of his mission to spread "the gospel of the Klan," appealing to those who were "100 percent anti-Catholic, anti-Jewish, anti-black, and 100 percent Protestant, white, and American-born."[174]

Meetings such as this one were not secret. They took place in the light of day, with full media exposure and advance advertisement. These were not the night riders of old. There were meetings held in churches and fraternal lodges. There were recruitment drives and Klan members openly proud of their membership. Election to Klan offices was widely reported in local newspapers as early as 1918. "At the Ku Klux Klan meeting on Saturday evening," readers of the *Daily News* learned in October of that year, "the election of officers for the coming six months took place."

The paper reported the names of the new local commander in chief (Dayton Wood), sergeant at arms (Bert Schultz), treasurer (Miss Bessie Johnson) and secretary (Miss Charlotte Warboys).[175]

This coverage reminds us of the Klan's appeal to those who thought that the modern America that was emerging after World War I was stressing too much individual freedom. "Aliens," or those who either did not belong to

Downtown Batavia in 1918, as the **KKK** began its ascendancy in the county.

KKK rally, probably in the Indian Falls region of the county, early 1920s.

Another KKK rally, most likely in Indian Falls, early 1920s.

KKK rally in Indian Falls, early 1920s.

Yet another KKK Indian Falls rally in the early 1920s.

KKK parade on Labor Day in Batavia, 1924.

Downtown Batavia at the height of KKK power in the county, 1924.

the Klan or were not sympathizers, constituted a threat to what the Klan referred to as "true" Americans. Resentment of those seemingly intent on destroying traditional America was what fueled Klan membership, and the subjects of this resentment were the targets of Klan rhetorical fury. These "aliens" had too much influence in the county, as the North Bergen Klan proclaimed in a public debate in 1918: "The subject was 'should the public good have preference to personal liberty?' The question was decided in favor of the affirmative."[176]

People doing damage to America were members of privileged groups who had taken control of the county—and America—from what the Klan considered "true Americans." This came out in clearly racial and religious terms, with the two categories typically merging. Catholics and Jews remained typical targets for county Klan members. As growing numbers of Irish and Italian Catholics entered Genesee County and began an upward social ascent, so too did the anger and resentment over perceived Catholic control. This anger sometimes manifested itself in physical threats to the Catholic communities in such places as Batavia, as reported in the *Daily News* at the time of the 1924 Klan-sponsored picnic: "Someone with white chalk marked large K's on the Summit Street side of St. Joseph's church and on the curb along the pavement yesterday. The Rev. William C. Kirby, rector of St. Anthony's Church, on Sunday morning told his Italian parishioners that the Klan had secured permission for using Exposition Park for a picnic and the use of the streets for the parade and he urged his people to conduct themselves quietly and to avoid starting any disorder."[177]

Catholics and Jews received blamed for a variety of social ills, ranging from corruption and crime through unscrupulous business practices to alcoholism and sexual immorality. The Klan fed on a wide range of anxieties. This enabled them to increase membership and build public support. These diverse concerns about the direction of post–World War I Genesee County produced a Klan that was more than an identifiable group. It was instead a broad social movement. People from many different occupations and social classes joined this movement in the 1920s. In addition, they were all fighting against different enemies. For example, there was Reverend L.E.H. Smith, known as the "raiding pastor." Klan members suspected that "aliens" bombed the home of this prohibitionist. As a result, anger over bootlegging—associated with both Jews and Catholics in Klan thinking—and bootleggers suspected of trying to kill a leader in the antiliquor movement translated into hundreds of Klan members and their sympathizers patrolling the highways to assist police in combatting the illicit traffic in liquor.[178]

Klan cooperation with local law enforcement translated into police officers who were themselves Klan members. This takes us into one of the central themes of this chapter. For a time, the Klan became mainstream in Genesee County, just as it did nationally in the 1920s. It fed off a variety of fears. Immigration, sexual immorality, political radicalism, ideas about evolution, the perceived threats of the pope in Rome, liberal Protestantism, world government, modern movies and art, and Judaism all constituted challenges to what was thought of as "real Americans." There was something here for different fears and resentments. The point in this chapter is not to condemn but rather to understand. In the process, we could reach a deeper understanding of our own day as we examine this aspect of Genesee County in the 1920s.

REAL AMERICANS

Because the number of African Americans in Genesee County remained low, the Klan did not concern itself with them apart from passing references in their literature and speeches. Along these lines, the Klan did not espouse a white supremacy designed to subjugate Black citizens. Their version of white supremacy was fashioned to intimidate non-Protestant whites, whom they believed engaged in treasonous criminal activities that could see America perish if not combatted. "On the night of November 6, 1924," we learn in an unpublished report prepared by Ruth McEvoy, the city of Batavia's historian in the early 1980s, "while Italians were celebrating Alfred E. Smith's reelection as Governor, three crosses were burned." Smith, an Irish Roman Catholic, symbolized for the Klan the twin evils of "Romanism" and foreign influence in American institutions. That he was openly supported by equally suspect Italian Catholics only fanned the flames of anger and resentment. "Old timers say that crosses were set up before the houses of prominent Catholic citizens," Ruth McEvoy wrote.[179] The degree of support for such actions within the county media cannot be determined, although such testimonies about cross burnings on private front lawns remained largely unreported throughout the mid-1920s.

The consistent rejection of Jews and Catholics in Klan literature was unlike the rejection of African Americans on racial grounds. Nevertheless, the desperate calls for excluding Jews and Catholics—and liberal Protestants—was part of the Klan definition of "100% American." The Klan believed that Jewish and Catholic offenses added up to an erosion of the United States and "Christian civilization." County Klan members viewed their role as sentries on patrol, guarding against pernicious forces threatening the Republic. They saw themselves as a good and pure civic movement responding to emergencies emerging in the county and the country at large in the 1920s.

The Klan viewed itself as being on a sacred mission. Protestantism and Klan beliefs remained inextricably bound together in Genesee County in the 1920s, and anyone outside of that could not really be an American. This message emanated from the pulpits of such churches as the South Alabama Baptist Church. At its April 27, 1924 service, seven "fully robed Klansmen, wearing their caps but without masks," approached the altar, where they remained during the service without incident after presenting a gift to the church."[180] Along with some Protestant churches, the Majestic Odd Fellows hosted a minister exiled from his pulpit in New York City because of Klan association. Reverend Oscar E. Haywood, on April 14, 1924, addressed a crowd of three hundred in Batavia. He spoke of the usual Klan concerns regarding residents born outside of the United States, the threat of Catholicism and Judaism, the immorality encouraged by

Hollywood movies, automobiles that allowed young people unprecedented privacy and the bootlegging of illegal liquor. By the end of Haywood's speech, an estimated one hundred county residents had joined the Klan.[181]

The "naturalization" of these residents into the Klan enabled them to recruit other potential Klansmen. The recruiters approached a candidate with an initial question: "Are you 100 percent for America?" The gathering at the Majestic Odd Fellows Hall was not the first of this kind. Two years earlier, the Odd Fellows had sponsored a talk by C.S. Fowler, the president of Atlanta's Lanier University and a national Klan organizer.[182]

Not all Protestant churches in Genesee County endorsed the Klan. The First Baptist Church, led by Reverend George K. Warren, was among those that denounced it. On the evening of November 26, 1922, Warren strongly repudiated "its principles and procedures." He attacked the oath of allegiance members were obligated to take. Pledging their loyalty to "the invisible empire was indefensible," Warren maintained. Instead, a true American's sole allegiance should be "to the law of the land, to the one flag." Any Klan actions otherwise invited the destruction of the very America Klan members professed to love. Noting the many farmers in the First Baptist Church, he likened Klan activities in the county to a farmer "who set fire to a pile of grain to get rid of the infesting rats and in doing so destroyed the grain, the barn and adjacent residence."

Even an opponent of the Klan such as Warren conceded that the Klan made valid points about alcohol abuse, governmental and corporate corruption, threats to the family resulting from sexual immorality, and the undemocratic nature of the Roman Catholic Church. Nonetheless, its methods, not to mention its earlier history of murder and violence, negated any good that the Klan could do in the community. Warren reminded his audience that "the federated Protestant churches" had gone on record in their opposition to the Klan, which encouraged the arousal of "racial prejudice and religious antipathies." He likened Klan attacks on Roman Catholicism to what was happening in places such as Oregon, where the Klan played an instrumental part in compelling Catholic parents to send their children to public schools to be "Americanized" when parochial schools were banned. He reminded the audience that the right of religious liberty was central to the Constitution.[183] Opponents of the Klan were pointing out that the Klan itself was hardly American.

Nonetheless, those drawn to the Klan continued to see it as the embodiment of "100 percent Americanism." For some, the attraction of the Klan lay in its seeming rejection of privilege, especially that exercised by economic and cultural elites. The Klan in this sense expressed another aspect of its "100 percent Americanism"—that of small entrepreneurs against the forces of economic bigness. Klan literature continuously exalted those who lacked economic power or education. This took a political turn, as politicians depicted as protecting the wealthy or the professional classes were viewed as aligning themselves against a democracy of mainstream businesspersons or nonprofessionals. The irony was that some of the leaders of the Klan were themselves, locally and nationally, people with more economic resources and greater professional standing. However, this contradiction was itself a strength of the Klan in the 1920s. There was something here for everyone.

This appeal to a broad cross section of people was clear in a list of Genesee County Klan members made public in the fall of 1924. In response to a court order in Buffalo, the names of county Klan members appeared in an edition of the *Rochester Evening Journal and the Post Express* on September 20, 1924. The occupations listed next to each name reveal how representative of county society the membership in the Klan was. Undoubtedly, each member brought his or her own resentments and anxieties to the decision to join. They also found some aspect of Klan ideology to be appealing. The list includes schoolteachers and bookkeepers from South Byron; mill hands and farmers from the town of Alabama; a mail carrier and a truck technician from Basom; butchers, sales clerks and students from Batavia; laborers and automobile dealers from Oakfield; and telephone operators and chauffeurs from Elba. Journalists, government workers, attorneys and physicians rounded out the list.[184]

The Klan believed that "real Americans" stood in opposition to concentrations of power. For the Klan, it did not matter where that concentration of power was. Protestantism was always dividing against itself, even on the question of the Klan. Decentralization of power was part of Protestantism and, hence, part of the Klan's worldview. In contrast, the Klan believed that there was only one "Romish" church. Those drawn to the Klan saw the pope as desiring world domination. The Klan believed Jews, though divided like Protestants, to be conspiring to achieve global domination through financial dealings and cultural control—for example, through Hollywood movies. "Real Americans" had only one allegiance—to the United States. This differed, the Klan believed, from immigrants, Catholics and Jews, whose loyalties lay elsewhere. These conceptions of "real Americans" spawned ideas about conspiracies serving to induce a fear driving county residents to join the

Klan. In Klan speeches, literature, and festivities, there was a predictable theme: the need for Anglo-Saxon Protestants to defend themselves and their institutions from people who were not really American. A poem that circulated in the county, entitled "Klippings, Komments, and Kriticisms," displayed the Klan view of those lacking the courage to wage a righteous war. A few lines suffice to demonstrate:

> *Y is for yellow,*
> *The color of him*
> *Who sold out his vote*
> *To old Rome for some gin.*[185]

Binding Anglo-Saxons together—not to mention attracting new members—required more than appeals to anxieties and resentments, however. There was also a place for fun and mystery. This, too, appeared in abundance in the Klan of Genesee County.

PARADES, CARNIVALS, GOOD FOOD, AND SECRETS

Klan parades, carnivals and community picnics appealed to potential recruits. They were characteristic of a decade in which large gatherings commonly served as entertainment. Like festive political conventions and Protestant camp meetings, Klan public events fostered a group identity.

In Genesee County, Klan events drew thousands of people. "Thousands of Persons Assembled for a Western New York Picnic," a headline in the *Daily News* reported. "Ku Klux Klansmen and Their Guests Gave Exposition Park and Vicinity Appearance of a County Day Fair." These festivities were very popular in the county throughout much of the 1920s. Not only were they attractive to those enjoying these festivals, but they also drew opponents of the Klan. This heightened the drama of open Klan activities. One anti-Klan activist in Batavia purposely parked his automobile directly in the path of a Klan parade. The police ordered him to move his vehicle. He did so by slowly making his way into the ranks of Klan marchers, "in an apparent effort to split the parade."[186]

In another case, a rumor circulated in Batavia that a man viewing a Klan parade suddenly emerged from the crowd and fired a gunshot through the door of an automobile in the parade before being disarmed and arrested. There was a subsequent controversy as to whether this event actually took place. On yet another occasion, the two-hour delay in the beginning of a parade was blamed on the intervention of New York governor Smith, who was at the time seeking the Democratic presidential nomination; this rumor proved to be unfounded.[187]

Public events such as these are reminders that there were two sides to the Klan. On the one hand, there was the cloak of secrecy manifesting itself in rituals, language, and the costume of the KKK. Conversely, there were the very public parades and carnivals. Both worked to attract people looking to belong to an organization that expressed its view on topics ranging from immigration through immorality to crime. Through parades and carnivals, the Klan strived to present the public image and experience of a social organization like many other fraternal groups that existed in the county in the 1920s. In the process, a public event such as a carnival provided income for the Klan.

The parades and carnivals attracted a variety of people, although these events were also avoided by people opposed to Klan beliefs. They were also reminders of what the Klan thought was being lost in modern America. Rides, music, various kinds of contests, and good food offered wholesome and innocent family fun. Flowers and crosses were visible on automobile floats. At the September 1924 fair in Batavia, vendors sold such items as Ku Klux Klan dolls. They also sold pinwheels and flags. The *Daily News* uncritically reported, "Numerous hot dog and refreshment stands were set up on the grounds and did a thriving business.…Klansmen and their guests made a real day's outing out of the affair, bringing their wives and children and other members of their families."

The same article covered the arrival of Dorothy Nichols, a Klan lecturer. When she arrived at the train station in Batavia, much was made of her doll, which was dressed in Ku Klux Klan robes, which media uncritically described. Signs with six-foot-high letters appeared in Albion and Medina directing traffic to the KKK event in Batavia. Mounted Klansmen maintained patrols on the carnival grounds, adding drama and excitement. It also attracted the curious, who paid twenty-five cents for admission to the carnival. (This was the price for men; women and children entered the grounds free of charge.)[188] The display of signage is indicative of local officials supportive of the Klan's racist message.

Tourists or people passing through on business who were drawn by the crowds thronging the event could apply for admission to the Klan festival on the spot by filling out a questionnaire with questions that included:

1. Are you Native-Born?
2. Are you an American Citizen?
3. Do you place America first?
4. Are you a Gentile who believes in White Supremacy?[189]

The bottom of this questionnaire included the phrase "Yours for America," followed by the signature "TI BO TIM." This mysterious acronym was a common feature of Klan literature in the 1920s. The Klan had its own language. This added to the sense of belonging felt by members, who saw themselves as waging a holy war against the evils besetting the county and the nation. While it is not clear what this acronym stood for, it is not surprising that it appeared. In Genesee County and elsewhere in the country, such acronyms as AYAK (Are you a Klansman?), AKIA (A Klansman I am), MIAFA (My interests are for America) and SANBOG (Strangers are near, be on guard) were all commonly used by Klan members.[190] The use of mysterious language combined with other practices to present the Klan as simply another fraternal organization, no different from the Rotary Club or the Elks. They, too, had their rituals and unique qualities. However, there were obvious differences between the Klan and the Rotarians or the Elks. Chief among these distinctions is the fact that in the 1920s, Rotarians and Elks did not burn crosses. The Klan may have held community picnics and carnivals, but they also engaged in other, less wholesome acts designed to entice recruits and intimidate enemies.

Why did the Klan burn crosses? Part of the answer lies in their proximity to Klan enemies. Even if such enemies had not violated the Klan's understanding of an acceptable political, economic, or racial order, the fiery cross communicated an explicit message—transgression could result in bad consequences. In the spring of 1924, a cross was burned in front of the courthouse in Batavia. Dissatisfied with the lack of progress made by the police in the investigation of a murder in Linden, some county residents understood the burning as one in which the Klan desired to take over the investigation if the police proved ineffectual.[191] In LeRoy, a Klansman distributed trinkets depicting fiery crosses. Automobiles marked with crosses appeared on county roads. These automobile crosses were made of pasteboard strips colored white and red. Off-duty Batavia police officers openly placed these crosses, about a foot in height and six inches in width, on the sides of these automobiles. In Indian Falls, "a huge fiery cross flickered on a hill top" accompanied by a band.[192]

Reports of burning crosses increased in frequency throughout Genesee County in the 1920s. Burning crosses appeared in East Pembroke, Pavilion, State Park, Austin Park, and in a local gravel pit. A burning cross also made an appearance at St. Joseph's Catholic Cemetery.[193]

Crosses were placed in proximity to a courthouse that was seen as embodying corruption and inefficiency, while in the case of St. Joseph's Cemetery, they were a very public expression of the necessity of mobilizing Protestants in an effort to rid the county of Roman Catholics. The Klan was issuing a general threat to Catholics: leave or face the consequences of remaining in Genesee County. Another message was also sent, warning those who were eligible to join the Klan but still hesitated. What could happen to white, Protestant, native-born residents daring to be outside of the "invisible empire"? What could happen to those who remained, in Klan parlance, "aliens"? Cross burnings produced nervousness and uncertainty for Catholics but also for Protestants who refused to join the Klan. Nevertheless, the threat of ostracism or violence could not be enough to induce one to join; there had to be positive inducements. Carnivals were one, but so, too, was the appeal throughout the 1920s of membership in a fraternal order—be it the Rotary Club or the Klan. Like those other associations, the Klan had to provide rewards of an emotional and financial nature for those willing to pay dues.

Just Another Club

By 1926, approximately 10.2 million Americans belonged to a variety of benevolent orders. To this number one can add another 500,000 children who belonged to affiliated groups.[194] Therefore, it is not surprising that the Klan adopted the same strategies for recruitment and retention that had proved successful for other groups in this period. Organizations such as the Rotary Club and the Elks offered the enticement of networking for those in business or seeking employment. This was especially important in an era long before the internet and, indeed, before many newspapers listed jobs in the classified section of their dailies.

Therefore, Klan meetings were regularly announced in local media. Media reports on Klan elections and other activities abounded. They were identical to articles concerning elections in other county groups. One could replace "Ku Klux Klan" with "Odd Fellows" and have a similar announcement. "Ku Klux Klan at North Bergen will meet at 8 o'clock

The Elks used this home in Batavia in 1920.

A fraternal group of Elks in the county, 1922.

on Saturday evening," an announcement in the *Daily News* reported.[195] A notice in that same newspaper five days later reported that at "a meeting of the Ku Klux Klan on Saturday" in North Bergen, "George J. Hottols was accepted as a member."[196] Other meetings in North Bergen made their appearance in the *Daily News* in March, April, and May 1918. A reader who was not familiar with the Klan could have assumed that it was simply another fraternal organization.

Like other organizations, there was a requirement to pay dues. "The Ku Klux Klan's treasurer on Saturday evening," one newspaper article revealed, "reported $4.50 on hand."[197] Business meetings teemed with descriptions of Klan activities. In North Bergen, there "will be a business meeting and election of officers of the Ku Klux Klan on Saturday evening," the *Daily News* reported in 1918.[198] Like other organizations, not everyone was willing to pay dues indefinitely—or even at all. In 1922, some people expressing an interest in joining the Klan were precluded because of an unwillingness, or inability, to pay dues. "Applicants were taken apart into groups," one account reads, "and some are said to have withdrawn when they learned that the initial donation of $10 was expected and that the full four degrees will cost $175."[199]

Even those who paid their initial dues were, in some cases, later disenchanted with Klan money management. Some members became angry after paying for robes that never arrived. Others complained of being pressured by Klan district leaders to purchase fireworks that they could not afford, echoing one man who stated, "I haven't got ten bucks" to join in the first place.[200] When some members discovered that one Klan district leader received two dollars for each new member enrolled, they quit the Klan in disgust. By one point in mid-1925, some "said openly that the Klan was fleecing the members."[201]

Like other fraternal organizations, there was concern about money management and the dues requirement. In other ways as well, the Klan in Genesee County resembled the fraternal orders of the 1920s. Here installation rituals and ceremonies replete with formalities and rules of conduct gave members a sense of belonging to an organization not open to everyone. The essence of Klan rituals was the creation of an aura of mystery. One description places new Klan members just south of the R.E. Chapin Farm in 1923: "It was said that a class of 200 was initiated at that time. The automobiles formed a circle lowering their lights into the center of the ring where initiation ceremonies took place."[202] In a manner eerily similar to the torchlight processions of Nazi storm troopers that arose less

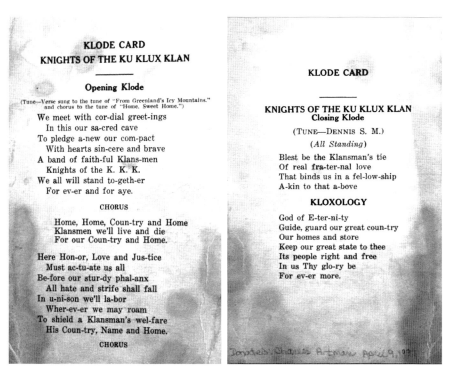

The front (*left*) and back (*right*) of a "Klode Kard" in Genesee County, early 1920s.

than a decade later in Germany, the initiation held at night gave entry into the Klan an aura of the sacred. Members saw themselves as holy fighters for true America in a dramatic and emotional way they did not experience in other fraternal orders. People with purpose joined together as Protestantism mobilized and militarized. Klan rhetoric intensified such spectacle. An excerpt from a "Klode Card," a postcard-sized creed designed to remind members of Klan beliefs, illustrates this. Members of the Knights of the Ku Klux Klan in Genesee County received this card throughout the 1920s:

We meet with cordial greetings
In this our sacred cave
To pledge anew our compact
With hearts sincere and brave
A band of faithful Klansmen
Knights of the K.K.K.
We all will stand together
Forever and for aye.

Home, Home, Country and Home
Klansmen we'll live and die
For our Country and Home.[203]

The anxieties and hatreds giving rise to Klan beliefs provided an emotional alternative to what many members saw as the blander nature of other fraternal orders. In addition, people drawn to a group with a history of violence and terror discovered camaraderie in the Klan. The existence of a password designed to exclude non-members from entering Klan meetings symbolized this.[204]

However, for the Klan to continue to grow, others who were angry and anxious about the direction the county was heading had to be attracted. Children in some measure were attracted by the Klan's promotion of baseball. While sporting events and carnivals drew children, there was still a concurrent need to interest more adults. Therefore, the Genesee County Klan sought women who were as angry and anxious as the men who joined the Klan. What role, then, did women play in the Klan of Genesee County in the 1920s?

WOMEN OF THE KLAN

Initially, the presence of women in Genesee County's Klan surprised me. Nevertheless, as I explored this aspect of the county's Klan history, I became less surprised. One of the major concerns of the Klan in the years following World War I was the moral direction America was heading. While the calendar read the 1920s, the culture of the county was still very much an embodiment of Victorian-era values. At the center of that worldview was the sanctity of the family, with women as the center of that family. The Klan in Genesee County welcomed the granting of the vote to women with the passage of the Nineteenth Amendment to the U.S. Constitution in 1920. The Klan supported the idea of female political participation since it meant participation by greater numbers of "100 percent Americans."

This meant that women had the opportunity to purify a county fast heading into immorality. The Klan believed the film industry to be dominated by Jews, an idea that was only confirmed for Batavia Klansmen by the fact that when the first movie theater opened in town in 1906, a Jewish man was part owner.[205] For the Klan, most movies were unacceptable for two reasons— they were immoral and they were Jewish. The Klan saw a conspiracy to weaken the morals of young people and, in the process, the family. As the primary protector of family life and community morals, women in the Klan saw themselves as righteous warriors for true Americanism. Armed with the vote and a tradition of political militancy reaching back into the nineteenth century, they moved headlong into Klan activism.

It is not surprising that they played an important role in Klan activity. Those who joined the group saw no contradiction between female church groups and Klan activity. "The Ku Klux Klan will meet in the church parlors at 8 p.m. on Saturday," a *Daily News* article told readers in 1917.[206] In North Bergen, an announcement for a "Ku Klux Klan Entertainment for the Rev. and Mrs. Smith" appeared. The committee in charge of this church luncheon included "Miss Bessie Johnson, Miss Alice Walker, and Miss Irene Merrill."[207] Numerous other announcements appeared showing churches and women of the Klan united in community activities between 1917 and 1924. One story in the *Daily News* in 1923, titled "Klan Services at South Alabama," included a photo that showed a gathering that included women at the South Alabama Church; hooded Klansmen were kneeling before the pulpit. Behind the pulpit was a large American flag and a "Welcome" sign. The caption to this photograph read, "This is a flashlight picture of the service at the South Alabama Baptist Church last Sunday evening during which seven members of the Ku Klux Klan, without masks, entered the church in the midst of the service and presented the pastor an envelope containing $35." The caption goes on: "The white-robed figures are seen kneeling before the altar while the Rev. David Brittain, pastor, offered prayer just before the presentation was made. The service had been announced as a community service and the church was filled."[208]

Klan women activists viewed their role as one of fulfilling a responsibility owed to their family and to society. They were conservatives seeking to uphold and restore what they viewed as traditional American values regarding morality in private and public life. Ironically, as activists they also insisted on leadership roles within the Klan that by their nature challenged male authority. It is not surprising that as the decade unfolded, they became increasingly prominent in county Klan activities. New officers emerged in the North Bergen Klan in 1918, and half of the leaders were women. Bessie Johnson was elected treasurer, while Charlotte Warboys became secretary. In that same year, Lelia Langdon accepted the office of treasurer of an auxiliary group, the Ku Klux Klan Society.[209]

The anxiety of Klan women was directed toward specific groups. Jews in particular received blame for subverting morality through such mediums as movies. Catholics remained targets as well. For example, the Klan insisted that women remained in convents against their will and that priests raped these women. "N is for nuns," one widely circulated flyer proclaimed, "those poor creatures confined in prison-house convents—'tis cert'nly unkind."[210] Yet the fears of immorality, especially female immorality, were also directed toward young Protestant women influenced by such new developments as movie houses and automobiles, for in both cases, couples were alone, unsupervised, and even in the dark. Apprehension produced by new inventions enabled newly enfranchised women to feel more certain about their need to play a role in Klan activism. Even if they were not seeking a Klan office, they could openly attend public Klan gatherings, as Clara Freeman from Alexander did in Batavia in the summer of 1924. Affirming her belief "in America first and White Supremacy at all times," she appeared at the 1924 Batavia fairgrounds picnic and expressed her support for the "Knights of the Ku Klux Klan," who "will speak upon the most powerful secret, nonpolitical and thoroughly American organization in existence. If You Hear the Rumblings in the Distance, you cannot afford to miss this opportunity. Don't judge this great law-abiding Order by hearsay. Come and hear the truth."[211] Like her male counterparts, Freeman saw the county as evenly divided between them and us, or between those who were "naturalized" (Klan members) and "aliens" (non-Klan people). The Klan assumed a veneer of normalcy serving to conceal its underlying mission, one linking it to the earlier Klan emerging in the South after the Civil War. For in the end, the Klan continued its struggle against forces deemed un-American, be they cultural, religious, political, or racial.

Are You With Us or Against Us?

The Ku Klux Klan in Genesee County did not always engage in activity normally associated with the Klan, except for the burning of crosses and hateful rhetoric. Evidence of lynching and whippings has not been found in the county's records. However, the legacy of white supremacy continued unabated. Rather than the few African Americans in the county, the Klan in Genesee County directed its efforts against other targets. Roman Catholics, Jews, and immigrants were the common targets of verbal assaults, warnings, and intimidation, primarily through a public presence of parades, carnivals, gatherings in churches, and, of course, cross burnings.

Non-Protestants, especially Irish and Italian Catholics, remained common enemies viewed as undermining the quality of life for "100 percent Americans." These groups, along with native-born Protestants who disagreed with Klan views, were associated with political corruption and other forms of criminal behavior, especially the sale and use of illegal liquor during this era of Prohibition. The struggle against perceived enemies of America was constant and unrelenting, and it was a dominant feature of county life throughout much of the 1920s.

This battle raged largely in the open. This was not the earlier Klan operating in the darkness of night. Public events were a regular feature of the Klan. Both men and women were open about their membership and commitment to the ideals of the Klan. Even those who did not join expressed their support, be it at church functions or what appeared to be harmless county fairs. As evidenced by occupations listed at enrollment, the Klan drew on many different occupations. This was a movement presenting itself as mainstream, as something straight out of the business district on Main Street in Batavia. Nevertheless, despite its efforts to be a radical version of the Elks, the Odd Fellows, the Masons, or even Rotary, they remained committed to ridding the county of their version of un-American people and ideas. Theirs was the local expression of the national movement of the Klan in the 1920s. The Klan for a time in the 1920s held great emotional appeal. While the Klan today is certainly not what it was in the 1920s, one can only speculate about just how much the sentiments drawing county residents to the Klan then are still apparent in the early twenty-first century.

CHAPTER 6

ACTIVISTS, FARM WOMEN, AND PROFESSIONALS

The fact that women were everywhere oppressed did not mean that their oppression was everywhere the same.
—*Chris Harman,* A People's History of the World

Women of various social classes experienced oppression in different ways. In this chapter, the focus is on women who possessed property, formal education, income, and the social status going along with these assets. They either wielded political power or retained access to those who did. These women were not as marginalized as their less privileged sisters, such as the impoverished or enslaved. These middle-class women cultivated methods to create an identity positioning them against restrictions society placed on them.

When they found themselves excluded, they fought efforts to subordinate them. They emerged as activists struggling for the abolition of slavery or the right of women to vote. Even when society demanded ideological conformity in such areas as domestic roles for married women, they quietly thought and read about new ways to conduct themselves within the home, as revealed by diaries kept by farm women. When reform within the constraints of marriage and family proved unworkable, they reached out publicly by taking the radical step of divorce. Still others sought to remain within socially demanded gender roles by entry into professions offering autonomy while avoiding the charge of radicalism. In some cases, middle-class homemakers avoided professions or political activism in lieu of membership in various social organizations. Regardless of their individual quest for some degree of independence, middle-class women in Genesee County felt deeply the wrongs they suffered by virtue of an accident of birth. In the quote here from a speech given at the LeRoy Women's Suffrage Meeting in 1885, the subject was suffrage, but the underlying sentiment appeared regardless of the tactic fashioned to achieve dignity and respect:

> *Ten millions of American citizens are defrauded of their birthright for the crime of being born women. I propose tonight to show our claim to this inheritance....The government of these United States is founded upon the power of suffrage—being founded upon this right every person born under this government is entitled to the right; in the case of men this is never disputed—black men were freed but to the black women and their white sisters, liberty is a mere negation.*[212]

Thirty-three years later, the dream of female suffrage in Genesee County became a reality, as described by LeRoy historian Lynne Belluscio: "On April 2nd, 1918, ninety-one year old Delia Philips became the first woman in LeRoy to vote. Five months earlier, on November 6th, 1917, the men of LeRoy voted against women's suffrage, but the amendment was passed in the State. So, at their first opportunity to vote, 58 women came to the Municipal Building to cast their ballots for village officers."[213]

The denial of voting was an example of public exclusion and oppression. Nevertheless, women also experienced a private oppression serving to stimulate strategies for coping and resistance. This is evident in the diaries kept by county women throughout the nineteenth century. Feelings of isolation and ideas about change abound in these diaries, as we shall see. "Very busy in kitchen," wrote Euogene L. Dewey of Byron in her diary entry of July 29, 1867. December 20 of that year saw no change, for she was "at home busy as usual."[214] Sylvina M. Green wrote despairingly in her diary entry of June 14, 1880, that she "froze last night…but cut blue cashmere dress for Genie." Along with "papering" the kitchen, she wrote of her effort in upholstering a seat on June 23 and upholstering yet another chair on July 12. The dreary quality of her private life continued in a diary entry of September 27, 1901, where she described with resignation a day in which she worked ceaselessly to can plums and pickle peaches.[215]

For these and other women, the domestic routine of hard work was broken up only by work outside of the home or participation in socially acceptable organizations, such as community or church groups. For some, there was also entry into political activism, such as the suffrage movement or, eventually, positions of political authority. Nevertheless, that last option generally came later, although there were exceptions in Genesee County even before World War I. These early movements into positions of public authority received comment from as far away as New York City. When Minnie Pfeifer moved into the role of acting Genesee County treasurer on December 7, 1907, the *New York Tribune* contained this editorial: "One by one women are invading the occupations popularly supported to be man's exclusive property. In Batavia, New York, a woman has held the office of County Treasurer for the last six months."[216]

County women navigated between a public presence taking various forms and a private life featuring equally demanding duties. Nevertheless, despite this tension, middle-class women reconciled private demands with involvement outside of the home. These women, excluded from such public arenas as politics, nonetheless developed associations inherently holding political implications. Prominent here was participation in the abolitionist movement, the suffrage movement and then the civil rights movement after World War II. Eventually, women occupied a growing number of elected offices in the county, where their public presence was obvious. We turn first to their abolitionist work in Genesee County in the years before the Civil War.

ABOLITIONISTS, SUFFRAGISTS, AND CIVIL RIGHTS

The antislavery movement in Genesee County, as in the nation as a whole, reveals a society ambivalent about the existence of republican values resting alongside chattel bondage. A long-standing revulsion regarding slavery made its appearance early on in the form of the county's participation in New York State's Colonization Society. In the fall of 1833, an article appeared in the *Republican Advocate* recommending the relocation of free African Americans to Africa as one way of "mitigating the evils of slavery." The writer added that this was not "the only measure which promises good to the African race." The ultimate resolution, then, is not colonization but the abolition of slavery: "We look upon slavery as a *wrong*, of which our nation is guilty. No circumstance…can justify its existence, or continuance. It seems highly desirable, therefore, that measures should be adopted with a view to *abolition*." This writer concluded that "whether colonization advances or recedes, we hope to see the efforts prospered of those who are endeavoring to effect the abolition of *slavery* in this land of *freedom.*"[217] County abolitionists condemned not only the inherent injustice of owning another human being but also, in addition, argued that slavery produced other crimes as well—such as kidnapping. In the summer of 1835, that same *Republican Advocate* in Batavia published accounts entitled "Kidnapping and Negro Stealing." In one account focusing on Natchez, Mississippi, readers learned that "Clary and Johnson were tried before the circuit court of the charge of negro-stealing, and were convicted. The punishment is death." The article added, "It appears from the evidence that Clary was caught in the act, by two gentlemen who blackened their faces, and whom he mistook for Negroes, and agreed to take to Texas for $125 each....Johnson was convicted of stealing a girl from Elijah Bell, Esq."[218]

The following month, the *Republican Advocate* offered a story about Reuben Crandall. He was "a white man" arrested "on a charge of circulating incendiary abolition pamphlets among the negroes" of Washington, D.C. His sister, "Miss Crandall," had "undertaken...to teach negro children in Connecticut."[219] While abolitionism was celebrated in the pages of the *Republican Advocate*, there remained, nonetheless, concern about the distribution of "incendiary publications." The anxiety here concerned producing heightened expectations regarding emancipation not easily met. From this perspective, the irony is that the situation of African Americans could worsen in the short run. Accordingly, "we say to the abolition gentlemen [to] keep your publications at home....You are, by your overzealous acts, doing an injury to the black population of the south which you will never be able to atone for. Their situation is miserable enough at best, but you, by your hot headed measures, are rendering it still more so."[220]

Hence, there appeared in the *Republican Advocate* in 1836 an announcement regarding an upcoming meeting of the Genesee County Anti-Slavery Society, scheduled for a week later. Concern over the effects of "fanatical" agitation, this announcement expressed the hope that "they will be allowed to hold their meeting in peace and quiet....We cannot think that anyone will be found so void of respect for the feelings of others...to disturb the tranquility of the Convention."[221]

Female opposition to slavery produced a demand for more public inclusion of middle-class women who had experienced a baptism of fire in the abolitionist movement and the risks involved in the writing and distribution of "incendiary publications." We might recall the 1848 Seneca Falls Convention petition, signed by "forty-four ladies of Genesee and

Wyoming," which called for "the repeal of certain laws" and in which these "married women…of the County of Genesee…respectfully represent" that "as women have never consented to, been represented in, or recognized by this government, it is evident that in justice no allegiance can be claimed from them." This call for the enlargement of female political participation was part of the unleashing of expanded horizons of freedom discernible in the abolitionist movement and intensifying during the Civil War. However, expanding female political participation developed surprising twists, as there were women in Genesee County, by the early twentieth century, who rejected the call for female suffrage and organized efforts to continue the policy of denying the vote to women.[222] More affluent women already enjoyed access to political leaders and were reluctant to expand that access to less affluent women through an extension of the vote. Others simply viewed politics as unethical and felt that women would lower their ethical standards if involved in the political process. An example of these views is the New York State Association Opposed to Woman's Suffrage.

This perspective appears in a March 1903 *Daily News* article titled "Anti-Women Suffrage." Readers learned of a public lecture scheduled in Batavia by Mrs. A.J. George of Massachusetts, a leader of the Women's Anti-Suffrage Association. Mrs. George spoke at the home of Mrs. L.L. Tozier on East Main Street. Although Mrs. Tozier supported women's suffrage, she nonetheless believed that those opposed to suffrage deserved to have their opinions aired.[223]

Debates over female suffrage continued through the early twentieth century. In June 1917, the *Daily News* carried stories of a suffrage convention scheduled in Ellicott Hall in Batavia. On "Women's Suffrage Meeting Day," Mrs. James Lees Laidlaw and Mrs. Frank J. Tone "were scheduled to speak in the eighth campaign district of the New York State Woman's Suffrage Party."[224] While this group advocated the right of women to vote, so, too, did the Bethany Grange, as described three months later in the *Daily News*. In an article headlined "Grangers of Bethany Endorsed Suffrage," readers learned that female suffragists from outside of Bethany also endorsed the resolution of the Grangers in Bethany Center, particularly those from the Stafford Grange.[225]

Nonetheless, that same *Daily News*, in the fall of 1917, published an advertisement in bold lettering: "Vote No on Suffrage." Within the context of war fever in the fall of 1917, the advertisement castigated Jeannette Rankin, the female member of Congress who had voted against U.S. entry into the First World War: "Woman Suffrage is responsible for Jeannette

Rankin, the woman congressman who votes against patriotic measures and defends the IWW [Industrial Workers of the World]. WOMAN SUFFRAGE is responsible for the picketing at the White House—an insult to good government. Woman Suffrage Must be Defeated in New York State. Vote No on suffrage."[226]

Regardless of where a woman stood on the question of female suffrage, the fact remains that both sides sought to place female leaders in a very public space. By 1920, with the passage of the Nineteenth Amendment to the U.S. Constitution, the question of voting rights for women became moot. The efforts of women in Genesee County to achieve greater participation in the political process became obsolete, at least in terms of voting rights. Nevertheless, another manifestation of female public presence appeared, and it grew out of the experience of the suffrage movement. This movement's impact was felt after World War II, when women played a key role in the birth of the modern civil rights movement.

The role of women in the modern civil rights movement found its most prominent expression in Genesee County churches. The Methodist Church played a key role here. Women's efforts here resembled the earlier struggles of the suffragists. In short, they worked to correct societal abuses, while remaining committed to the general framework of American society. This was especially the case in a largely conservative Genesee County, so it is not surprising that a clear manifestation of the civil rights movement in the county was that of the Methodist Church.

An example of this is the *Official Journal and Yearbook of the Western New York Annual Conference of the United Methodist Church* in 1969. In a report it included titled "Christian Social Concerns," a priority was the effort to reduce "prejudice and racial strife." Methodist women sought this through the development of educational programs called "brotherhood schools" in Genesee County. The objective of these programs was to "help reduce prejudice and inter-racial tensions within individual Christians." The public presence of women involved in the brotherhood school movement through a "Women's Society" revealed women in a variety of settings, as described in the *Official Journal and Yearbook* of 1969: "A group within a local congregation may desire a 'Brotherhood School' in a one-evening setting, or a full weekend, a Sunday morning setting with Church School and the regular Sunday service, or a Sunday evening youth program. The local congregation may want to have this Brotherhood School in their own church, on a retreat weekend, or in an inner-city setting away from their local church building."[227]

The array of brotherhood school settings did not match the dramatically different offices women held in the county for decades. This assortment of political and commercial offices not only reveals the medley of public roles occupied by county women but also illustrates just how early this kind of public presence began to develop. While we have already seen Pfeiffer assuming the role of acting Genesee County treasurer as early as 1907, the *Progressive Batavian*, in 1888, featured an article titled "A Woman Bank Director." Mrs. Adelaide Kenny, the daughter of business leader Dean Richmond, became the first woman bank director in western New York.[228] These two women are early examples of women successfully moving into visible niches of public presence. This trend continued well beyond 1888 and 1907, and it is a reminder of the different public roles some middle-class women played.

A short time before the entry of the United States into World War II, Mrs. Maud Homelius of Batavia became that city's first female mayor. On November 28, 1941, she took the oath of office. Her husband, Frank H. Homelius, had died in the mayor's office of heart disease. Concerned about the immediate need for a mayor's signature on bond interest and payroll checks, the city council selected her from a list of three candidates.[229] Ironically, Mrs. Homelius died from heart disease while still serving as Batavia's mayor three years later.

Over the years, women served in numerous capacities as elected officials. June Cotton Vukman became Batavia's first female member of the town council in 1985 and, two years later, won the position of town supervisor.[230] In the spring of 1979, Mary J. Chilson was elected to the Oakfield Village board, making her the first woman ever elected to the role.[231] The *Democrat and Chronicle* portrayed Florence Gioia in a long 1991 article as her constituents' "tireless advocate" while serving in the Genesee County legislature.[232] These were some of the women holding elected office in Genesee County, a pattern continuing to this day. While enjoying the status of elected office accompanying such a public presence, the question nonetheless remains: did women still experience private injustices as in earlier times? Some insights are possible by looking at some of the civil disputes and diaries found in the county.

FARM WOMEN AND SOME OF THEIR THOUGHTS

The Genesee County History Department Archives contains large numbers of diaries kept by women. These diaries contain personal reflections that yield insights into some of the private feelings of the women who wrote them. The advantage of diaries for the historian is that they tend to provide descriptions and yearnings not always found in official documents, which are more guarded in nature.

These diaries hold great historical significance precisely because their blunt quality suggests how women responded to the conditions of their time and place—responses inherently more guarded in a less private setting. An excellent illustration of how *resistance* took place among middle-class women is a diary in the Genesee County Archives dating from 1887. This writer, the unnamed mother of Genie D. Green, accepted many of the social conventions of middle-class life in her day. She also displayed efforts to smuggle into her middle-class world ideas whose ultimate effect was the undermining of that self-satisfied Victorian perspective. Genie's mother longed for a release from a universe that she simultaneously embraced and found stifling. On January 24, 1887, she wrote, "There are periods in our lives when some new book or acquaintance comes to us like an added sun in the heavens, lighting the darkest places and chasing every shadow away." For numerous days after this entry, she spoke of drudgery—"doing odd jobs." Then an unexpected and particularly long entry appeared. On June 1, 1887, she wrote excitedly of how light illuminates dark places: "For [my] eighty ninth birthday I can best honor it by consecrating myself to work for every good." What was this "every good"? It was "for the enfranchisement of women...for progressive thought and for moral and spiritual growth and development."[233]

Many of her entries focused on feminist books or lectures. Later in the year, she spoke of reading a biography of the eighteenth-century feminist Mary Wollstonecraft, author of the 1792 work titled *A Vindication of the Rights of Woman*. Three days later, she wrote enthusiastically of meeting a Cleveland artist "who has made a clay bust of Miss Susan B. Anthony," the national leader of the women's suffrage movement. Her reading and lecture attendance continued to indicate a dissatisfaction with the world women inhabited in 1887. By September 1887, she displayed an interest in the writings of Josiah Strong, the Protestant minister who was a leader in the social gospel movement, which sought to combat poverty, alcoholism, crime and other social ills. She wrote of her study of Strong's *Our Country and Its Possible Future, and Its Present Crisis*.[234] Much of her remaining diary entries exhibit much the same—her deep desire to light the dark places in a woman's life.

FEMALE DISCONTENT
AT HOME ENTERS COUNTY COURTS

Nevertheless, recording despair in one's private life—and then keeping those reflections hidden in a diary—was not always possible or even desirable. Women sometimes expressed discontent publicly, and nowhere was this more evident than in civil cases involving women in Genesee County. One case in particular captures both legal and private realities faced by women. In the case of *Francis M. Walsworth and One v. Sarah A. Walsworth and Others*, the issue of marriage and property holding appears. This 1896 case, conducted in the Supreme Court of Genesee County, provides insights into economic relations married women found themselves in as America entered the twentieth century.

In *Walsworth*, a disputed lien produced lengthy interrogatories disclosing the intricacies of marriage and its connection to property and contractual rights. The very existence of marriage depended on solemnization; an informal union did not exist for legal purposes. Therefore, *Walsworth* provides a detailed examination of the ceremony constituting a bona fide marriage. The court found that "marriages may be solemnized by any justice of the peace in the county in which he is chosen; and they may be solemnized throughout the state by any minister of the gospel, who has been ordained according to the usages of his denomination, who resides within this state, and continues to preach the gospel." This section includes a discussion of the issuance of the marriage certificate, the names and addresses of at least two witnesses to the marriage and the requirement of a justice or a minister to keep a record of the marriages performed, along with copies of the certificates issued that were filed with the county clerk.[235]

Having established the existence of a bona fide marriage in *Walsworth*, the principles of gender equality in marriage also emerges. In what began as an action concerning a lien on real property eventually emerges, in the interrogatories, as an illustration of how both husband and wife shared in the management of property. Nevertheless, a woman disagreeing about *how* that property is managed is one who may have to resort to legal action in order to assert rights already established through legislation and prior court decisions. Such management could become complicated if a partner to the marriage made property decisions pursuant to the wishes of a third party not enjoying the rights attendant to a bona fide marriage but who, nevertheless, influenced the decisions of someone who was part of a bona fide marriage. This appears in the interrogatories contained in *Walsworth*:

"Was there a time when Walter Cheney left his wife, Helen Godfrey, and if so, where were they living at the time, and about what time did he leave her? If you do not know the date, fix it by the ages of his children or by any other fact or circumstance in your mind." The interrogatories continued: "Did you keep up your acquaintance with his wife, Helen Godfrey, and did you see her from time to time after the said Walter Cheney left her, and if so, did he ever live with her after he left her."[236]

Walsworth is a reminder that a woman owning property—while enjoying that right—could nonetheless find it affected by a third party, whose actions disturb both the marital relationship and the necessity of managing property. There remained a gap between the public presence of a married woman owning real property and the private anguish of seeing that right threatened and, hence, having to use the courts to reassert a right she already possessed. It remained irrelevant whether the married adulterer was cohabiting with a third party. What mattered more was whether the economic management of a married couple's jointly owned real property remained threatened by that third party's influence. The public presence of a woman owning real property was weakened by the private reality of third-party influence.[237]

It is not surprising that some women simply opted out of marriage altogether. In some cases, even if married, they pursued a public presence in which marriage did not become a priority in their lives. Such a perspective ushers us into the world of female educators and clergy in Genesee County from the nineteenth century on.

Female Professionals

While some female teachers married in the nineteenth and early twentieth centuries, most did not. By the 1840s, women began entering teaching in growing numbers. Well into the twentieth century, elementary school teachers were predominately female. They were viewed by many as surrogate mothers. Female teachers had the duty to rear children with sound character. Historian of education Ruth M. Elson has written, "The purpose of nineteenth-century American public schools was to train citizens in character and proper principles. Most textbook writers had an exalted idea of their function; almost all made statements such as the following: 'The mind of the child is like soft wax to receive an impression, but like the rigid marble to retain it.'" Elson reminds us that educators

Seventh-grade class at Batavia's Union School, 1888. The teacher is unidentified.

"were much more concerned with the child's moral development than with the development of his mind." She adds, "The important problem for nineteenth-century American educators was to mold wax in virtue rather than in learning."[238]

Despite demands for moral instruction, low salaries, and the moral clauses of teacher contracts, female teachers viewed their work as offering a degree of independence and upward social mobility not found elsewhere. Genesee County fit into this national trend. In Batavia, Miss Smead of Pavilion eventually assumed control of a private school until later relocating to Toledo, Ohio, where she continued to teach in another school. Between 1875 and 1889, Miss E.G. Thrall operated a school in Batavia.[239]

By 1848, records reveal the existence of the Byron Young Ladies School. An art school was also located in Byron, and the painting teacher was Julia M. Hall. In LeRoy, Ingham University served as a shining example of female education, both in terms of student enrollment and in the production of female educators. Ingham was the first women's college in New York State, offering a bona fide college curriculum providing instruction to young women. Madame Staunton led a faculty of seventeen professors and a support staff. Eventually, about eight thousand students graduated from Ingham and taught at colleges ranging from Vassar through Wellesley to the University of Rochester.[240] This was a group of women whose training

Top: Another unidentified teacher with her second-grade class at the Washington Street School in Batavia in 1888.

Bottom: Teacher Margaret McGurk with her class in Batavia, year and school unknown.

at Ingham, not to mention their teaching duties, remained dramatically different from that of most female teachers. Most female teachers worked in the county's elementary schools, which meant a very different work environment.

Ester Sprout administered the first school in Stafford in 1806. This was a private school, as the New York State legislature did not establish free public schools until 1849. By 1867, a public school was operating in Stafford, led by Alida Randall. Florence Leanen was the teacher in this school by 1914. Clara Rudolph then taught there between 1925 and 1938. Lila Page subsequently followed her. This school closed in the 1940s, when Stafford students began to be bussed to schools in LeRoy.[241]

Women becoming schoolteachers used the limited opportunities provided by teaching to carve out a niche that afforded a measure of independence, while still subscribing to the norms expected of women in the nineteenth and much of the twentieth centuries.[242] They bore a striking resemblance to those women who ventured into other professions permitting a measure of independence while avoiding the charge of "radical" feminism. Those other women, resisting gender norms in a conservative fashion, were the female clergy of Genesee County.

Female clergy in the county are part of a long line of Protestant ministers stretching back to Clarissa Danforth, the first woman ordained in the Free

Another kind of professional. St. Jerome's Hospital nurses in Batavia, sometime in the 1920s.

Will Baptist denomination in New England.[243] In 1893, Frankie Cook began her service as the pastor for Alexander's Universalist Church. In Batavia, at the Friends Church, Mary Jane Weaver served as the first evangelist. Anna Leggett then followed her. Grace Shephard served as the church's third pastor between 1929 and 1934. In 1982, Marie King became pastor of the East Bethany Presbyterian church.[244]

Female clergy such as these represent a trend in which women exerted a public presence—and wielded public power—outside of politics per se. They expressed power outside of elected office. Female clergy, like female educators, understood that activities not explicitly political nonetheless affected the political process. Theirs was a moral authority apparent in classrooms, lecture halls and churches. They refused to be ignored and attacked efforts to subjugate them in a very public way. But other women developed other ways to challenge the status quo. It is to them we now turn.

Women's Organizations in Genesee County and the Subtle Resistance to the "Cult of Domesticity"

Historians have used the phrase "cult of domesticity" since the late 1960s to describe a middle-class family structure that first emerged in the early 1820s. Its legacy persisted after that, and traces of it remain today. It emerged with a dramatic shift in the economy translating into a middle-class family not having to produce goods in order to survive. Instead, wives and children remained at home while husbands and fathers labored outside of the home producing services and commodities demanded by society.

Men supported the family by earning income. There were two spheres delineated along gender lines here. One sphere contained a man and his work outside the home. The other realm was that of a woman, who only periodically ventured into the outside world. Her concern was the home and the family. It did not take long for an attendant view to develop: a woman was delicate and vulnerable—forces outside of that front door could easily victimize her.

This ideology of the nuclear family appeared in a variety of sources, including newspapers, novels, religious publications, magazines, and advice books. An integral part of the description was the idealization of the "good" woman—one remaining pious, sexually pure, focused on home

Interior of a middle-class home in Batavia around 1900.

Another photograph of a Batavia middle-class home around 1900.

A woman in opposition to the "cult of domesticity." Shown here is Mrs. Wren, the first female telegraph operator from Genesee County (Stafford). This photograph was taken around 1886.

and family and submissive to men. Piety meant that women possessed an innate religiosity, one working to improve the world through compassion and love. Sexual purity meant the avoidance of the label "fallen woman," or one whose virginity was lost before marriage. Ironically, it was in this area that a woman exercised what some called a great deal of superiority and power, for men were compelled to remain in control of their own sexual desires—a benefit, it was believed at the time, to society as a whole.

Submissiveness to men was in actuality an acknowledgment of what men were supposed to be—anything but submissive. Men were supposed to be active; they were doers. Conversely, women were encouraged to be passive beings who accepted subordination to duty, to what life presented, to God and, of course, to men. It was believed that women should display a consistent spirit of obedience, pliability, and humility. The cult of domesticity promoted housework and childrearing as uplifting tasks—not as limiting ones that kept women out of the business, professional or political worlds. Indeed, any activity keeping a woman in the home—such as needlepoint—

Young women publicly displaying the "cult of domesticity." *From left to right*: Florence Dolbeer, Elizabeth Carney, Ruth Mason, and Fanny Day, Batavia High School students, celebrating George Washington's birthday in 1899.

emerged as the natural promotion of a cheerful, peaceful home to which men looked forward to returning. As one scholar put it, for men home was "a haven in a heartless world."[245]

FEMALE ACTIVISM THROUGH SOCIAL ORGANIZATIONS

Despite the enormous social pressures to promote these assumptions, women throughout the nation, and in Genesee County, developed forms of resistance that took them out of the home and gave them a sense of empowerment. Organizations taking women outside of the home included the Batavia Concert Band, the Genesee Symphony Orchestra, and the

Ladies Auxiliary of the Alexander Fire Department. The landmark Society of Genesee County, the LeRoy Historical Society, and the Wednesday Study Club were also some of the organizations taking county women beyond the confines of domesticity.[246] This last group is a good example of women pushing the boundaries set by the "cult of domesticity" further and further out. Francis Pratt Douglas and Emma Comstock founded the Study Club in October 1904. Its stated purpose was to "promote intellectual development, a broader view of all subjects and to stimulate social intercourse." One local history noted that the Study Club was "patterned after other women's organizations formed around the turn of the century. These organizations took shape as a result of a national movement wherein educated women were interested in maintaining intellectual pursuits once their formal education was completed. Early members of the Wednesday Study Club were recruited to form a varied representation of women in the community: married and unmarried working outside and within the home, with differing professions and interests."[247]

As seen in the Wednesday Study Club, the ideal of middle-class women throughout the history of the county is the model of seriousness. Regardless of the roles played by women in that history, there is an underlying and consistent theme of purpose. The insistence on purpose was routinely smuggled into wider society in ways not immediately detectable. The patience that this required sometimes, however, gave rise to expressions of private grievances taking a very public—and surprising—form.

Despite the achievement of leadership roles in Genesee County, middle-class women suffered discrimination. Regardless of the obstacles they faced, they persisted in the effort to be a part of the political and economic system of the county rather than going too far beyond it. In the process, they resisted social expectations. They endured discrimination and yet pushed against the social boundaries surrounding them. They sought methods designed to undermine seemingly impregnable bastions of male authority functioning to impede the attainment of a more fulfilling life. Women in Genesee County struggled against a society not allowing them the full development of their potential.

But the descriptions of women in this chapter are hardly the final word on middle-class womanhood in county history. Instead, the story of women in the county was a complex unfolding of the ways they adjusted to social change instead of trying to escape from it. Personal adjustments, political and cultural compromises and the efforts to construct new identities all stood as painful reminders that women, in their public presence or in their battles with private injustices, sought to resolve the tension between social expectations and personal aspirations. Between 1802 and our own day, there remained a consistent effort to work out compromises between traditional expectations and modern sensibilities. How this dynamic will ultimately be resolved is unknown. However, one thing is certain. The experience of many middle-class women reminds us what barriers exist to individual fulfillment within, and beyond, Genesee County.

CONCLUSION

The longest histories ever written leave out far more than they put in.
—*N. T. Wright,* Paul: A Biography

I started to write this book wondering where to begin. I now end it wondering where to stop. There remains so much to write. Nonetheless, I consciously selected areas of the county's past serving to illuminate the reality faced by people living there. This is admittedly not a traditional history, as I did not confine myself exclusively to events or to an orderly chronological span of time. Genesee County's history is a long stretch of time punctuated by specific realities. Those realities were influenced by the national events addressed in this book. In turn, local perceptions of those events shaped the understanding of nationwide phenomena. Hence, I looked at leaders who fell through assassinations. There was the possibility of nuclear war, and immigrants fashioned identities within the context of an identity as a Genesee County resident.

Social movements took people in different directions. Middle-class women struggled to ensure their place in county society. Woven through all of this were constants uniting people in Genesee County. This brings us to a central and final point.

There was an underlying continuity in the county's history. While much changed since 1802, much also remained the same. The history of the county remained anchored in a belief in individual liberty. The enlargement of individual liberty was viewed as the cornerstone of a good life. As I stressed in chapter 4, even at the depths of the Great Depression, the majority of people in Genesee County voted for candidates suspicious of extensive government intervention in the life of a person. The recent COVID-19 crisis was analogous to the economic downturn of the 1930s in this regard—county residents in general remained suspicious, if not openly hostile, to heavy-handed governmental policies.[248] Despite orders to maintain social distancing, Batavia High School football players insisted on helping members of the community. As a local sportswriter put it, "Although they're not in season, the Batavia football team, along with its head coach, has been doing its best to provide for others." In this article, Head Coach Brennan Briggs added this: "In this state of panic, I think it's important that as a community we help those that are in need." Helping "those that are in need" included the team's "offering of services for any elderly person in need of an errand."[249]

Therefore, neither the Great Depression nor COVID-19 weakened the value of *individualism*, as described in chapter 4, which is so apparent in county history. There was always a place for governmental authority, so long as that authority did not tread too heavily, or too long, on individual freedom. The individual person retained primacy in the long history of Genesee County, regardless of the winds of change swirling around the individual. As we look ahead, a central question for the county remains: Will the belief in individual liberty continue to characterize Genesee County as it moves deeper into the twenty-first century and beyond?

NOTES

Preface

1. Robert A. Gross, *The Minutemen and Their World* (New York: Hill and Wang, 1976).
2. Genesee County Historians Association, *Genesee County, New York: 20th Century-in-Review and Family Histories* (Nashville, TN: Turner Publishing Company, 2004), 11–12.
3. Genesee County Historians Association, *Genesee County, New York*, 13.
4. An example here is Mary McCulley, ed., *History of Genesee County, New York, 1890–1982* (Interlaken, NY: Heart of the Lakes Publishing, 1985).
5. A useful treatment of local history is Carol Kammen's *On Doing Local History*, 2nd ed. (New York: AltaMira Press, 2003).

Chapter 1

6. *Daily News*, "Normalcy Returning to Area After President's Funeral, Many Attend Rites in City," November 26, 1963, 1.
7. *Daily News*, "Not Sick," June 8, 1968, 2.
8. *Daily News*, "Long, Long Time," April 6, 1968, 2.
9. A brilliant and extremely detailed book about President Kennedy's assassination and the Warren Commission is Vincent Bugliosi, *Reclaiming History: The Assassination of President John F. Kennedy* (New York: W.W. Norton, 2007).

10. *Daily News*, "Why? Is Still Unanswered Question," September 30, 1964, 2.

11. *Daily News*, "Shock and Disbelief Mark News of the Assassination as Batavians Learn of Death," November 23, 1963, 1.

12. *Daily News*, "Shock Wave of President Kennedy's Death Engulfs High and Low throughout World," November 23, 1963, 4.

13. Ibid.

14. *Daily News*, "Events Cancelled," November 23, 1963, 1; "Stock Exchange Closing Monday," November 23, 1963, 4.

15. *Daily News*, "Stores Close Until 2 P.M. on Monday," November 23, 1963, 1; "Schools Close, Some Offices Will Be Shut," November 23, 1963, 1.

16. *Daily News*, "TV Programming Resumes Tuesday," November 25, 1963, 1.

17. *Daily News*, "Normalcy Returning to Area after President's Funeral, Many Attend Rites in City Tragic Weekend Comes to Close, Business Resumes," November 26, 1963, 1.

18. *Daily News*, November 25, 1963, 22.

19. *Daily News*, "At Midnight, Mrs. Kennedy Goes to Husband's Grave with a Sprig of Flowers," November 26, 1963, 1.

20. Jessica Mitford, *The American Way of Death* (New York: Simon and Schuster, 1963).

21. Speech of President Kennedy at the University of Washington on November 16, 1961, JFK Library, https://www.jfklibrary.org/learn/about-jfk/historic-speeches/address-at-university-of-washington.

22. *Daily News*, "Let Us Gather," November 27, 1963, 2.

23. *Daily News*, "Assassination Problems Different Now," December 6, 1963, 2.

24. *Daily News*, "China's Bomb Widens U.S. Defense Role," October 17, 1964, 1.

25. *Daily News*, "Whole Country Sick, Wounding of RFK Shocks Area Residents," June 5, 1968, 1.

26. *Daily News*, "County Area Shares Grief in Tragedy," June 6, 1968, 1.

27. Ibid.

28. *Daily News*, "Whole Country Sick," 4.

29. *Daily News*, "Robert F. Kennedy—the All-Out Candidate," June 5, 1968, 4.

30. Ibid., 1, 4.

31. Quoted in William L. O'Neill, *Coming Apart: An Informal History of America in the 1960s* (Chicago: Quadrangle Books, 1971), 373.

32. O'Neill, *Coming Apart*.

33. Quoted in Denise Anderson and Jan Edmiston, "MLK Weekend: A Call to Action," Presbyterian Church USA, January 12, 2017, https://www.

pcusa.org/news/2017/1/12/mlk-weekend-call-action. See also Rick Perlstein, *Nixonland* (New York: Scribner, 2009), 249–51.

34. "Senator Robert F. Kennedy Speaks after the Assassination of Reverend Martin Luther King, Jr.," in William Safire, ed., *Lend Me Your Ears: Great Speeches in History* (New York: W. W. Norton, 1992), 198.

35. *Daily News*, "Racial at a Glance," April 5, 1968, 1.

36. *Daily News*, "Chicago Wracked by Night-Long Siege of Terror," April 6, 1968, 1.

37. David W. Noble, David A. Horowitz and Peter N. Carroll, *Twentieth Century Limited*, vol. 2, *America, World War Two to the Present* (Boston: Houghton Mifflin, 1980), 478.

38. O'Neill, *Coming Apart*, 181.

39. *Daily News*, April 6, 1968, 2.

40. *Daily News*, "Area Schools to Remain in Session," April 8, 1968, 1.

41. *Daily News*, "Nation Respectful; in Tribute to Dr. King," April 9, 1968, 1.

42. *Daily News*, "Low-Income Housing Termed Moral Duty by City Businessman," April 9, 1968, 1.

43. *Daily News*, April 9, 1968, 2.

44. *Daily News*, "On the Racial Scene," April 9, 1968, 1. Batavia had the largest number of African Americans in the county, estimated to be about five hundred. See Ruth M. McEvoy, *History of the City of Batavia* (Batavia, NY: Hodgins Printing, 1993), 256. Relevant reading here is Michael Kazin and Maurice Isserman, *America Divided: The Civil War of the 1960s* (New York: Oxford University Press, 2007).

45. *Daily News*, "Riots Disrupt Easter in Some Sectors," April 10, 1968, 3.

46. Martin Luther King Jr., "Martin Luther King's Nobel Prize Acceptance Speech" December 10, 1964, Nobel Prize Internet Archive, http://www.nobelprizes.com/nobel/peace/MLK-nobel.html.

47. *Daily News*, "Even If They Kill Us, We Still Have Power," April 5, 1968, 1.

48. Quoted in Noble, Horowitz and Carroll, *Twentieth Century Limited*, 474.

49. *Daily News*, "Air Force, Civilian Views Differ on Bomb Defenses," April 25, 1968, 1.

Chapter 2

50. *Daily News*, "Emergency, Firefighting Forces Go to Aid of Veterans Hospital to Combat Simulated 'Disaster,'" September 14, 1956, 1;

"Post Office Shattered by 'Bomb,' Quick Shift Made to VA Hospital," September 15, 1956, 1.

51. The literature regarding the Cold War is extensive. However, there are a few succinct monographs introducing readers to this crucial moment in American history. They include J.P.D. Dunbabin, *The Cold War: The Great Powers and Their Allies* (London: Longman, 1994), and Brian T. Brown, *Someone Is Out to Get Us: A Not So Brief History of Cold War Paranoia and Madness* (New York: Grand Central Publishing, 2019). The fears of communism were also rooted in the tyranny of communist governments. See Stephane Courtois, "The Crimes of Communism," in Stéphane Courtois et al., eds., *The Black Book of Communism: Crimes, Terror, Repression* (Cambridge, MA: Harvard University Press, 1999), 1,031. The author reminds us that communists killed about 100 million people worldwide between 1917 and 1999. Also see Andrew Bacevich, *The Limits of Power: The End of American Exceptionalism* (New York: Hold, 2008) and Richard Powers, *Not without Honor: The History of American Anticommunism* (New Haven: Yale University Press, 1998).

52. Clifford Geertz, "Thick Description: Toward an Interpretive Theory of Culture," in Clifford Geertz, *The Interpretation of Cultures* (New York: Basic Books, 1973), 3–30.

53. See "President Dwight D. Eisenhower Takes His Leave with a Surprising Theme," in William Safire, ed., *Lend Me Your Ears: Great Speeches in History* (New York: W.W. Norton, 1992), 381.

54. "President Dwight D. Eisenhower Takes His Leave," 381.

55. The cultural emphasis on the danger posed by the Soviet Union is described in Brown, *Someone Is Out to Get Us*. See also Kyle Cuordileone, *Manhood and American Political Culture in the Cold War* (New York: Routledge, 2005).

56. *Daily News*, "Airman from Oakfield Expects Duty in Korea," October 15, 1953, 23.

57. *Daily News*, "Corfuran in Army Arrives in Korea," October 14, 1953, 12, and "Soldiers from Area Training in Korea," October 24, 1953, 7.

58. *Daily News*, "Batavia Soldier's Body Arriving on Saturday, to Be Met by Escort," October 29, 1953, 4.

59. *Daily News*, "Body of Batavian Is Found in Korea, Cpl. Norman F. Smart Earlier Was Listed as Missing," December 5, 1953, 1.

60. *Daily News*, "Ex-Batavian, First Said Missing, Dies in Communist Prison Camp," November 13, 1953, 1.

61. *Daily News*, "Russian 'Ran the Show' in Korea Says Released Batavia Officer, Declares Will to Live Saved Him," October 31, 1953, 1.

62. *Daily News*, "Capt. Preston Warns of Communist Peril in Rochester Talk," November 7, 1953, 4.

63. *Daily News*, "War in Korea Still Goes On," June 25, 1953, 2.

64. *Daily News*, "School Drills Wise Procedure," October 15, 1953, 2.

65. *Daily News*, "Public Schools Set to Launch Atom Bomb Drills Next Week," October 23, 1953, 1.

66. *Daily News*, "Hospital Readies War Disaster Plans," October 23, 1953, 9.

67. *Daily News*, "Not Entitled to Sympathy," September 3, 1953, 2.

68. *Daily News*, "Good News," September 5, 1953, 2; "House Probers Say Miss Ball Never a Member of Red party," September 12, 1953, 1. Instructive here is Elaine T. May's *Homeward Bound: American Families in the Cold War Era* (New York: Basic Books, 1999).

69. *Daily News*, "Clergyman by Adopting Slogan Helped to Speed Demobilization," September 15, 1953, 1. By 1953, this had become a common theme in some circles. See, for example, Elizabeth Dilling, *The Red Network: A "Who's Who" and Handbook of Radicalism for Patriots* (Kenilworth, IL: self-published, 1936), 21–27.

70. *Daily News*, "Be on Guard Best Policy," September 18, 1953, 2; *I Married a Communist* appeared in 1949 as the Cold War deepened. *I Was a Communist for the F.B.I.* was released two years later.

71. *Daily News*, "Memorial Dedication at Oakfield Church," December 24, 1953, 14.

72. Herman Kahn, *On Thermonuclear War* (Princeton, NJ: Princeton University Press, 1961). See also Fred Kaplan, *The Wizards of Armageddon* (Redwood City, CA: Stanford University, 1991).

73. Henry Kissinger, *Nuclear Weapons and Foreign Policy* (New York: W.W. Norton, 1969).

74. For a graphic image of a post–nuclear war world, see Jonathan Schell, *The Fate of the Earth* (New York: Alfred Knopf, 1982).

75. *Daily News*, "Leave for Military Duty," October 11, 1956, 9. A relevant monograph here is Elaine T. May's *Fortress America: How We Embraced Fear and Abandoned Democracy* (New York: Basic Books, 2017).

76. *Daily News*, "Genesee County Young Men," September 1, 1956, 5.

77. *Daily News*, "Most County Doctors Aid in Civil Defense," September 1, 1956, 4.

78. *Daily News*, "Preparing for Disaster," September 13, 1956, 1. The inclusion of Catholic nuns on the coordinating committee is not surprising, as the Roman Catholic Church in this period remained vehemently anticommunist. The Catholic anticommunist crusade included such

things as a comic book for children, titled *The Red Iceberg*. Sponsored by the Catholic Catechetical Guild, it was distributed to Catholic schoolchildren.

79. See a county media summary in *Daily News*, "Emergency, Firefighting Forces," 1; "Post Office Shattered by 'Bomb,'" 2.

80. New York State Civil Defense Commission, *State of New York Operational Survival Plan*, New York State Civil Defense Commission subject files, New York State Archives, series no. 13125.

81. A relevant article here is Matthew Connely et al., "'General, I Have Fought Just as Many Nuclear Wars as You Have': Forecasts, Future Scenarios, and the Politics of Armageddon," *American Historical Review* 117, no. 5 (December 2012): 1,431–60.

82. Dwight Eisenhower, *Mandate for Change: The White House Years, a Personal Account* (Garden City, NY: Doubleday, 1963), 145.

Chapter 3

83. A good summary of the county's ethnic diversity resulting from immigration comes from Ruth McEvoy, "Ethnic Make-Up," in *History of the City of Batavia*, 251–57.

84. McEvoy, "Ethnic Make-Up," 251. See also Thomas Sowell, "The Irish," in *Ethnic America: A History* (New York: Basic Books, 1981), 23–24.

85. For a succinct interpretation of the American culture forming the foundation for assimilation, see Arthur Schlessinger Jr., *The Disuniting of America: Reflections on a Multicultural Society* (New York: W.W. Norton, 1993), 27–28. The dark side of assimilation is explored in John Higham, *Strangers in the Land: Patterns of American Nativism, 1860–1925* (New Brunswick, NJ: Rutgers University Press, 2002). Also see Donna Gabaccia, *Foreign Relations: American Immigration in Global Perspective* (Princeton, NJ: Princeton University Press, 2012); David R. Roediger, *The Wages of Whiteness: Race and the Making of the American Working Class* (London: Verso, 1991); and Roediger, *Working Toward Whiteness: How America's Immigrants Became White: The Strange Journey from Ellis Island to the Suburbs* (New York: Basic Books, 2005).

86. McEvoy, "Ethnic Make-Up," 251–52; Patrick McGreevy, *Stairway to Empire: Lockport, the Erie Canal, and the Shaping of America* (Albany: State University of New York Press, 2009), 103.

87. "Saint Peter's Parish," unpublished history located in the Genesee County History Department Archives, n.d., 1.

88. Good introductions here include R.F. Foster, *Modern Ireland, 1600–1972* (New York: Penguin Books, 1989); Sowell, "The Irish," 17–42; William Shannon, *The American Irish: A Political and Social Portrait* (Amherst: University of Massachusetts Press, 1989); and Kirby Miller, *Emigrants and Exiles: Ireland and the Irish Exodus to North America* (New York: Oxford University Press, 1985).
89. Sowell, "The Irish," 19–20.
90. Foster, *Modern Ireland*, 318–44.
91. *Republican Advocate*, "Dreadful Famine in Ireland," May 12, 1846, 3.
92. *Republican Advocate*, "Relief for Ireland!," February 23, 1847, 2. See also, for example, "The Famine in Ireland," *Republican Advocate*, May 25, 1847, 2; "The Irish and Famine," *Republican Advocate*, November 30, 1847, 1.
93. *Spirit of the Times*, "The Row on the Canal Near Lockport," April 6, 1852, 2.
94. In the aforementioned issue of the *Spirit of the Times*, an article on the same page alerted readers concerned about Catholicism in western New York about a priest in Ireland convicted of destroying a portion of the Bible. Readers learned that a Roman Catholic priest has been prosecuted, to conviction, in the county of Mayo, Ireland, for burning publicly a copy of the Holy Scriptures as a "Book of the Devil."
95. *Republican Advocate*, "Sisters of Charity," August 7, 1849, 2. In the same issue, on the same page, a Roman Catholic was congratulated for his efforts to remove alcohol from American life—a movement favored by many native-born Protestants in this period. See "Father Matthew at Work in Boston."
96. "Saint Peter's Parish," 2.
97. McEvoy, "Ethnic Make-Up," 251.
98. McCulley, *History of Genesee County*, 111.
99. There is a voluminous literature on Italian immigration and American reaction to it. Good introductions include Sowell, "The Italians," 100–129; Higham, *Strangers in the Land*; Concetta A. Chiacchio, "Current Patterns of Socialization and Adaptation in an Italian American Community" (EdD diss., Rutgers University, 1985); Richard Gambino, *Blood of My Blood: The Dilemma of the Italian Americans* (Garden City, NY: Doubleday, 1974); Salvatore J. LaGumina, *WOP!: A Documentary History of Anti-Italian Discrimination in the United States* (Toronto: Guernica, 1999); Andrew Rolle, *The Italian Americans: Troubled Roots* (Norman: University of Oklahoma Press, 1984); and Jerre Mangione and Ben Morreale, *La Storia: Five Centuries of the Italian American Experience* (New York: Harper Perennial,

1992). Some of my writings here include *Between Peasant and Urban Villager: Italian Americans of New Jersey and New York, 1880–1980—The Structures of Counter-Discourse* (New York: Peter Lang, 1993); "Italian Americans and the Question of Assimilation," in Alfred J. Wrobel and Michael J. Eula, eds., *American Ethnics and Minorities: Readings in Ethnic History* (Dubuque, IA: Kendall/Hunt Publishing Company, 1990), 165–79; and *Western New York Heritage*, "Becoming American: The Journey of Italians in Genesee County" (Winter 2018): 52–61. Also refer to the Paolo Busti Cultural Foundation Executive Committee, *The Legacy of Italian-Americans in Genesee County, New York* (Interlaken, NY: Heart of the Lakes Publishing, 1992), 20, 30; McEvoy, "Ethnic Make-Up," 252; and Department of Rural Sociology, *The People of Genesee County, New York: Trends in Human Resources and Their Characteristics, 1900–1960*, Bulletin no. 62-18 (Ithaca, NY: Cornell University Press, 1963).

100. Quoted in Rolle, *Italian Americans*, 3.

101. This perspective is thoughtfully articulated in John P. Diggins, *Mussolini and Fascism: The View from America* (Princeton, NJ: Princeton University Press, 1972), 5–21.

102. *Spirit of the Times*, "Pompeii," May 13, 1825, 2.

103. Diggins, *Mussolini and Fascism*, 7.

104. An interesting though sanitized company history is Tom Foley, *United States Gypsum: A Company History, 1902–1994* (USG Corporation, 1995).

105. McCulley, *History of Genesee County*, 248; Foley, *United States Gypsum*, x, 248.

106. *Daily News*, "Two Men Killed in Gypsum Mine," November 2, 1905, 1.

107. *Daily News*, "Miners at Oakfield Laid Down Shovels, Accident Caused 200 Italians to Quit Work," November 3, 1905, 1.

108. *Daily News*, "Miners at Oakfield Making Disturbance," December 15, 1905, 1.

109. *Daily News*, "Five Miners Taken at Oakfield Mill, Stolen Goods Found in the Boarding House," December 16, 1905, 1, 6.

110. *Daily News*, "Gypsum Company Procuring Arms, Men Who Will Not Work at the Oakfield Plant Will Be Driven Off," September 12, 1906, 1.

111. Just one of many examples of this was *Daily News*, "Oakfield Italian Robbed His Friend," November 2, 1905, 4. In neighboring New Jersey, stereotypes about alleged Italian immigrant criminality also abounded in such newspapers as the *Paterson Morning Call* and the *Newark Evening News*. Also consult Mangione and Morreale, *La Storia*, 340, and Steven J. Ross, *Working-Class Hollywood: Silent Film and the Shaping of Class in America* (Princeton, NJ: Princeton University Press, 2000).

112. *Daily News*, "Ku Klux Klan Gatherings," August 15, 1924, 2. Relevant here is the consideration of the Klan on a national level in Linda Gordon, *The Second Coming of the KKK: The Ku Klux Klan of the 1920s and the American Political Tradition* (New York: Liveright Publishing, 2017).

113. *Daily News*, "New Jersey Klan Ceremony Interrupted by a Picnic," August 18, 1924, 1.

114. *Daily News*, "Midnight Procession of Klansmen Moved from Batavia to Indian Falls for Ku Klux Klan Initiation Ceremonies," August 19, 1924, 1.

115. *Daily News*, "Thousands of Klansmen Are to Hold a Picnic Labor Day in Batavia," August 21, 1924, 1.

116. *Daily News*, "Use of Park by the Klan Meeting with Opposition upon the Part of Some," August 23, 1924, 1.

117. *Daily News*, "Ku Klux Klansmen and Their Guests Gave Exposition Park and Vicinity Appearance of a County Fair Day," September 2, 1924, 1–2. Four years later, a Roman Catholic priest received a postcard in which the writer told him, "Go to Rome, or we'll get you." A copy of this postcard is located in the Genesee County History Department Archives, postmarked in Buffalo on November 6, 1928.

118. See the summary of this lynching in Mangione and Morreale, *La Storia*, 200–213.

119. *Daily News*, "Klan Is Outlawed in New York State, Supreme Court Justice Revokes Charter of Hooded Organization on Fraud," July 30, 1946, 1.

120. *Daily News*, "Rural Resourcefulness," August 17, 1946, 2.

121. *Daily News*, "Bumper Onion Harvest Under Way," August 21, 1946, 5.

122. *Daily News*, "Blind Veteran Operates Farm Like Batavian Intends to Do," August 26, 1946, 1.

123. *Daily News*, "Batavian Builds Onion Topper," August 24, 1946, 8.

124. Eric Martone, ed., *Italian Americans: The History and Culture of a People* (Santa Barbara, CA: ABC-CLIO, 2017), 148. Also see Gary R. Mormino, ed., *The Impact of World War II on Italian Americans, 1935–Present* (New York: American Italian Historical Association, 2007).

125. A good biography of Basilone is James Brady, *Hero of the Pacific: The Life of Marine Legend John Basilone* (Nashville, TN: Turner, 2010).

126. *Daily News*, "Back-Home Spaghetti Treat in Korean War," May 3, 1952, 1; "B-29 Crewman Back from Korea Ten Days After Bombing Mill," June 4, 1952, 1; "Del Plato to Run as an Independent," June 13, 1952, 6; "Batavian Is Graduate of Fredonia College," June 14, 1952, 4;

"New Social Security Officer Is Assigned to Batavia Territory," June 18, 1952, 7.

127. *Daily News*, "At 80 Years Old—Mr. Rosica Is Busy Every Day as Shoe Cutter," March 28, 1973, 1.

Chapter 4

128. *Daily News*, "Mr. Hoover Becomes President Amid Record-Breaking Acclaim of Host," March 4, 1929, 1; "President Hoover's Speech Today Bristled with the Epigrammatic," March 4, 1929, 1.

129. *Daily News*, "Strikers Denounce Wages of $8.90 a Week," March 21, 1929, 12.

130. *Daily News*, "Stock Market Broke Wide Open—Sales Expected to Exceed All Records—Call Money Jumping Up to 20 Per Cent," March 26, 1929, 1.

131. *Daily News*, "Grand Jury Indicted Bergen's Ex-Banker," February 12, 1930, 1.

132. *Daily News*, "Hume MacPherson, Bergen Native, Killed Wife with Ax, then Himself, Money Troubles Probable Cause," April 19, 1930, 1.

133. *Daily News*, "Reward—Bank Bandits—Dead or Alive," July 17, 1930, 10. This advertisement occupied a full one-fourth of page 10.

134. *Daily News*, "Wyoming Man Earns Living by Peddling Candy in Coat Cart," December 11, 1930, 1. In just this one issue, there are numerous stories about the poverty gripping the county. Batavia police distributed money to the "needy"; brokers were compelled to suspend operations; a mother murdered two of her children because she was "crazed by poverty and fearful of the future of her four children"; cartoons depicted hungry children staring through the window of a butcher's shop; and a woman was escorted out of Batavia because she was "selling a lotion." She told the police that she had "several children she was supporting."

135. *Daily News*, "400 Under-Nourished Children Largely in Families Whose Parents Are Too Proud to Ask for Aid Will Receive Help from the Red Cross," December 7, 1931, 7.

136. *Daily News*, "Man Who Stole Sheep Pleads He Was Hungry," December 21, 1931, 6.

137. *Daily News*, "Shirt Workers Went on Strike—Two Hundred Women and Girls Object to Cut at a Batavia Factory," January 25, 1932, 6.

138. *Daily News*, "Services in Church Sunday at Bethany," July 8, 1932, 4.

139. The ballot is shown in a full-page presentation, *Daily News*, "To the Voters of the City of Batavia and Towns of Alabama, Alexander, Batavia, Bergen, Bethany, Darien, Elba, LeRoy, Oakfield and Stafford," November 7, 1932, 7.

140. *Daily News*, "Voting Rush in This City Near Record," November 8, 1932, 1.

141. *Daily News*, "Tremendous Victory for the Democrats Pictured as the Late Returns Drift In," a headline positioned alongside "Wadsworth and Weller Win in Contests, Genesee Holds Fast to Republican Party," November 9, 1932, 1.

142. *Daily News*, "Career of Herbert Clark Hoover Told to Readers at a Glance," June 15, 1928, 5.

143. *Daily News*, "Hoover's Parents—Old Home," June 15, 1928, 9.

144. *Daily News*, "Herbert Hoover's Birthplace," June 20, 1928, 9.

145. "Resolution Regarding President Hoover," in *Genesee Annual Conference of the Methodist Episcopal Church* (Rochester, NY, 1932), 30.

146. *Daily News*, "Go to the Polls!," November 4, 1932, 2.

147. Franklin D. Roosevelt commencement address, Oglethorpe University, Atlanta, George, May 22, 1932, https://publicpolicy.pepperdine.edu/academics/research/faculty-research/new-deal/roosevelt-speeches/fro52232.htm.

148. Roosevelt speech to the Commonwealth Club of San Francisco, September 23, 1932, Public Policy, https://publicpolicy.pepperdine.edu/academics/research/faculty-research/new-deal/roosevelt-speeches/fro92332.htm.

149. *Daily News*, "Every Bank in County Opened for Business," March 15, 1933, 1.

150. *Daily News*, "State Highway Work Relief Plan Welcome News to Genesee People," March 18, 1933, 1.

151. *Daily News*, "Last Car of Flour Received in City," March 20, 1933, 4.

152. *Daily News*, "Three Hundred Family Men Will Work for State Next Week," May 6, 1933, 1.

153. *Daily News*, "A Letter to the Public—Spirited People of Batavia," August 23, 1933, 4.

154. *Daily News*, "Report of Cost Account System Showed Farms Lost Money in '32," August 23, 1933, 5.

155. *Daily News*, "Big Republican Parade," October 29, 1936, 12.

156. *Daily News*, "Thoroughly American," October 31, 1936, 2.

157. *Daily News*, "Keep Going with Roosevelt," alongside of the Republican "Where Your $1 Goes," October 31, 8–9.

158. The pattern of some areas of the country remaining Republican in the 1936 election is discussed in David Pietrusza's fine book, titled *Roosevelt Sweeps Nation: FDR's 1936 Landslide and the Triumph of the Liberal Ideal* (New York: Diversion Publishing, 2022), especially 205.

159. McEvoy, *History of the City of Batavia*, 246.

160. *Daily News*, "A Few Impressions," November 5, 1936, 2.

161. Will Lissner, "Black Legion Men Held Without Bail; On Murder Charge; Judge Calls Killing of Poole Michigan's 'Most Striking Crime' in 25 Years," *New York Times*, May 26, 1936, 1; Robert Goldston, *The Great Depression: The United States in the Thirties* (New York: Bobbs-Merrill Company, 1968), especially 190. Also see Bradley W. Hart, *Hitler's American Friends: The Third Reich's Supporters in the United States* (New York: St. Martin's Press, 2018), and Charles Gallagher, *Nazis of Copley Square: The Forgotten Story of the Christian Front* (Cambridge, MA: Harvard University Press, 2021).

162. *Daily News*, "Two Systems of Rule," October 6, 1938, 2.

163. *Daily News*, "Let's Get Together," October 7, 1938, 2.

164. *Daily News*, "Let's Be Americans," October 19, 1938, 2.

165. *Daily News*, "Bund Meeting Ban Looms After Crowd Drops Man in Pond," October 11, 1938, 1.

166. *Daily News*, "Kiwanis Speaker Hits Communism," October 14, 1938, 7.

167. *Daily News*, "The World's Business," November 14, 1938, 2.

168. *Daily News*, "How to Beat the Reds," December 23, 1938, 2.

169. *Daily News*, "Candidate Willkie Says F.D.R. Leading the Country into War; Spoke on Big Government Costs," October 16, 1940, 1, 5.

170. *Daily News*, "Willkie Fears U.S. Socialism in F.D.R. Trend," October 19, 1940.

171. As an example, see the discussion of a Republican women's group during the first year of the Roosevelt administration, as described in *Daily News*, "Republican Conference Speaker Charged NRA Is Communistic," October 30, 1933, 5.

Chapter 5

172. Department of Rural Sociology, *The People of Genesee County, New York: Trends in Human Resources and Their Characteristics, 1900–1960*, Bulletin no. 62-18 (Ithaca, NY: Cornell University Press, 1963), 19.

173. "Ku Klux Klansmen and Their Guests," 1.

174. Ruth McEvoy, unpublished report, 1982, Genesee County History Archives, 391.

175. *Daily News*, "Ku Klux Klan Held Its Semi-Annual Election Saturday," October 9, 1918, 7.

176. Ibid.

177. "Ku Klux Klansmen and Their Guests," 1.

178. *Daily News*, "K.K.K. to Patrol Road for Bootleggers," April 25, 1924, 2.

179. McEvoy, unpublished report, 1982, 392.

180. *Daily News*, "Klansmen without Their Masks Visited South Alabama Church, Presented a Purse to Pastor," April 28, 1924, n.p.

181. *Daily News*, "Ku Klux Klan Speaker Addressed 300 in Batavia," April 15, 1924, n.p.

182. *Daily News*, "Batavia Ku Klux Klan Branch Starting with Fifty Members Heard Address of Potentate," November 17, 1922, n.p.

183. *Daily News*, "Principles of Ku Klux Klan Denounced from the Pulpit by the Rev. George K. Warren," November 27, 1922, n.p.

184. "Batavia Klan Officers Named" and "Genesee County Names Found on Klan List," *Rochester Evening Journal and the Post Express*, September 20, 1924, 1. See also "Western New York and Buffalo List K.K.K.," pamphlet (n.d.), housed in the Genesee County History Archives.

185. A.W.K., "Klippings, Komments, and Kriticisms," *The Good Citizen*, housed in the Genesee County History Archives, n.d., n.p.

186. "Ku Klux Klansmen and Their Guests," 1.

187. Ibid.

188. Ibid.

189. "Form P-220," Admission Questionnaire, Knights of the Ku Klux Klan, Genesee County, New York, housed in the Genesee County History Archives.

190. A good overview here is Gordon, *Second Coming of the KKK*, 73.

191. *Daily News*, "Flaming Cross Planted Close to Courthouse," April 8, 1924, n.p.

192. *Daily News*, "Fiery Cross on a Hill," August 19, 1924, n.p.

193. McEvoy, unpublished report, 1982, 393.

194. Gordon, *Second Coming of the KKK*, 30. See also Mary Ann Clawson, *Constructing Brotherhood: Class, Gender, and Fraternalism* (Princeton, NJ: Princeton University Press, 1989).

195. *Daily News*, September 13, 1917, 6.

196. *Daily News*, September 18, 1917, 3.

197. *Daily News*, "Ku Klux Klan's Finances," n.d., n.p.

198. Untitled announcement, March 7, 1918, 2.

199. *Daily News*, "Batavia Ku Klux Klan Branch."
200. Lois M. Brockway and Shirley F. Kern, *Ku Klux Klan Activities, Town of Pembroke, 1923–1924*, unpublished report, 1981, Genesee County History Archives, n.p. This comment was offered in response to a question concerning his refusal to become a member of the Klan in 1924.
201. McEvoy, unpublished report, 1982, Genesee County History Archives, 394.
202. *Daily News*, "Ku Klux Klan Conducted Initiation Ceremonies," October 15, 1923, n.p.
203. "Klode Card," n.d., housed in the Genesee County History Archives.
204. Brockway and Kern, *Ku Klux Klan Activities*, n.p.
205. McEvoy, *History of the City of Batavia*, 62.
206. *Daily News*, "Ladies' Missionary Society and the Ku Klux Klan This Week" (no specific date in 1917), n.p.
207. Undated and unlabeled announcement housed in the Genesee County History Archives, n.p.
208. *Daily News*, "Klan Services at South Alabama" (no specific date in 1923), n.p.
209. *Daily News*, "North Bergen Officers" (no specific date in 1918), n.p.; announcement in the *Daily News*, March 20, 1918, 9.
210. A.W.K., "Klipings, Komments, and Kriticisms," n.d., n.p.
211. "Form P-220," questionnaire, Knights of the Ku Klux Klan, Genesee County, New York, housed in the Genesee County History Archives.

Chapter 6

212. "Excerpt from a Speech Given at the LeRoy Women's Suffrage Meeting in 1885," *Welcome Card of the LeRoy Historical Society*, April 2, 2018, 3.
213. Lynne Belluscio, *Welcome Card of the LeRoy Historical Society*, April 2, 2018.
214. Diary of Euogene L. Dewey, July 29, 1867; December 20, 1867, Genesee County History Department Archives, Shelf Location 29.b.2.2, 12.01 DEW 0135.
215. Diary of Sylvina M. Green, January 26, 1880; September 27, 1901, Genesee County History Department Archives, Shelf Location 29.B.2.2. 12.01 GRE 0146.
216. Quoted in Susan L. Conklin, "Women's History: Women in Politics in Genesee County," unpublished history, March 2007, Genesee County History Department Archives, 3.

217. *Republican Advocate*, "Colonization," October 22, 1833, 1.

218. *Republican Advocate*, "Kidnapping and Negro Stealing," July 28, 1835, 2.

219. *Republican Advocate*, "Fanatics Behold Your Work," August 25, 1835, 1.

220. *Republican Advocate*, "Incendiary Publications," August 25, 1835, 2.

221. *Republican Advocate*, March 8, 1836, 2.

222. "State of New York, No. 129, In Assembly, March 15, 1848, Petition," 1, Genesee County History Department Archives. An important work here that sheds light on the connection between female abolitionists, the eventual end to slavery and the construction of female political identity, is Susan Zaeske's *Signatures of Citizenship: Petitioning, Antislavery, and Women's Political Identity* (Chapel Hill: University of North Carolina Press, 2003).

223. *Daily News*, "Anti-Woman Suffrage, Meeting Will Be Held in Batavia at the Home of Mrs. L.L. Tozier," March 7, 1903, n.p.

224. *Daily News*, "Woman Suffrage Meeting Day," June 1, 1917, 7.

225. *Daily News*, "Grangers of Bethany Endorsed Suffrage," September 7, 1917, 2.

226. *Daily News*, "Vote No on Suffrage," October 29, 1917, 8.

227. *Official Journal and Yearbook of the Western New York Annual Conference of the United Methodist Church* (North Chili, NY: Roberts Wesleyan College, 1969), 121.

228. *Progressive Batavian*, "A Woman Bank Director," January 27, 1888, 3.

229. *Daily News*, "Mrs. Maud Homelius Appointed to Succeed Her Late Husband; First Woman Mayor of Batavia," November 28, 1941, 1.

230. Barb Miller, "June Cotton Vukman the First Councilwoman Elected to the Batavia Town Board," unpublished history, March 1998, Genesee County History Department Archives.

231. Al McWilliams, "Elect First Woman to Oakfield Board," *Daily News*, March 21, 1979, 1.

232. *Democrat and Chronicle*, "Friend, Battler and Watchdog," March 31, 1991, n.p.

233. Diary of the mother of Genie D. Green, January 24, 1887, and June 1, 1887, Genesee County History Department Archives, Shelf Location 29.B.2.2. 12.01 GRE 0143.

234. Diary of the mother of Genie D. Green, September 6, 1887; September 9, 1887; September 13, 1887.

235. *Francis M. Walsworth and One v. Sarah A. Walsworth and Others*, Supreme Court, Genesee County (1896), section 6, 7–17; Genesee County History Department Archives, Court Records, Shelf Location 59.A.3, 12.06.

236. *Francis M. Walsworth and Arthur Ostrander v. Sarah A. Walsworth and Others*, Supreme Court, Genesee County (1896), 3; Genesee County History Department Archives, Court Records, Shelf Location 59.A.3, 12.06.
237. An overview of complexities faced by wives in property disputes and its connection to marriage is offered in Mary Ann Glendon, *The Transformation of Family Law: State, Law, and Family in the United States and Western Europe* (Chicago: University of Chicago Press, 1989).
238. Ruth Miller Elson, *Guardians of Tradition: American Schoolbooks of the Nineteenth Century* (Lincoln: University of Nebraska Press, 1964), 1.
239. McCulley, *History of Genesee County*, 72, 122.
240. Ibid., 157, 212–13.
241. Ibid., 318.
242. In 1902, the average monthly salary paid to Genesee County teachers stood at $40.12. Even adjusted for 1902 wages, this is a very low salary. Teachers in LeRoy received the highest monthly salary at $47.00. The poorest paid county teachers taught in Alexander, making only $34.80 per month. See "Proceedings of the Board of Supervisors," November 26, 1902, Genesee County History Department Archives.
243. A fascinating biographical sketch of Reverend Danforth is in Reverends G.A. Burgess and J.T. Ward, *Free Baptist Cyclopedia, Historical and Biographical* (Chicago: Woman's Temperance Publication Association, 1889), 148.
244. McCulley, *History of Genesee County*, 39, 54, 144.
245. Christopher Lasch, *Haven in a Heartless World: The Family Besieged* (New York: W.W. Norton, 1995).
246. See the overviews of these groups in *Genesee County, New York: 20th Century-in-Review and Family Histories* (Nashville, TN: turner Publishing Company, 2004), 163, 179.
247. *Genesee County, New York*, 179.

Conclusion

248. Those coercive state and medical mechanisms are explored in detail in Robert F. Kennedy Jr., *The Real Anthony Fauci: Bill Gates, Big Pharma, and the Global War on Democracy and Public Health* (New York: Skyhorse Publishing, 2021). A relevant book here is Jefferson Cowie, *Freedoms Dominion: A Saga of White Resentment to Federal Power* (New York: Basic Books, 2022).
249. Alex Brasky, "Even in a Pandemic, Local Sports Teams Stay Rational, Helpful," *Daily News*, March 17, 2020, B2.

About the Author

Michael J. Eula is the Genesee County, New York Historian and a Professor Emeritus of History at El Camino College. He is the author of more than thirty articles and books in American and European history, including *Between Peasant and Urban Villager: Italian-Americans of New Jersey and New York, 1880 to 1980—The Structures of Counter-Discourse*. His articles have appeared in such journals as *Air University Review*, *Differentia: Review of Italian Thought*, *Religion*, *The History Teacher*, and *Italian Americana*. His awards include being named a National Endowment for the Humanities Fellow three times, along with receiving the DeAngelis Prize in History in 2000. He is an honors graduate of Rutgers and the Regent University School of Law, where he received an LLM degree. He holds an MA and a PhD in history from the University of California–Irvine. A disabled veteran, he lives in the Town of Batavia, New York, with his wife, Allison; their cats, Penny and Holly; and four parakeets. They have three children, Jason, Catie, and Lizzie.

Visit us at
www.historypress.com